Praise for *Soaring A*

"This amazing book about codepen[...] and empowering. We don't have to stay stuck in unhealthy patterns. We can all cut the cord and soar. Freedom at last!"

-Susan Jeffers, Ph.D., author of *Feel the Fear and Do It Anyway* and *Embracing Uncertainty*

"In Lisa's *Soaring Above Co-Addiction* the reader can find answers written in her straight forward style that apply to real life problems. This book would appeal, not only to those dealing with an addict, but those living in the shadow of another waiting for someone to make them happy. Through her personal stories, and the stories of others, Lisa shares how you can take your life back no matter what is going on around you. Real solutions to real problems…great!"

-Barb Rogers, author of *If I Die Before I Wake*

"*Soaring Above Co-Addiction* is an amazing narrative that will lift the mind and raise the spirit of every reader. Lisa effectively integrates timeless wisdom, spiritual concepts, and proven recovery techniques into a format designed to help you overcome fear and take back your life"

-Brian McAlister, author of *Creating a Personal Action Plan for Life Beyond Sobriety*

"Incredibly readable and refreshingly honest. This book will be of great benefit, not only to those suffering from co-addiction, but to anyone facing adversity"

-Mark Meincke, award winning author of *Why Not Me? The keys to unlock your power and release your potential*

Praise for *Soaring Above Co-Addiction*

"In this enlightening and down-to-earth book, Lisa reveals a treasure trove of possibilities to the reader who may feel hopeless, beaten down and defeated. Through her own real-life example, she takes us on her journey of creative discovery and ultimate victory—in spite of the odds that were stacked against her.

Lisa leads by example...showing how you can understand and empathize—but not enable your loved-one, walk away from a situation without anger, take control and finally feel good about yourself.

This book is packed with hundreds of practical, and easy to implement tips for being prepared—so that you have a plan-of-action, no matter what. Once a person realizes that they really can control how they react to these outside influences, positive changes happen and a new sense of calm and confidence are born.

Soaring Above Co-Addiction is a much-needed book that fills a void in this genre of literature and will be treasured by many."

-Joe Herzanek, author of the award winning book *Why Don't They Just Quit? What families and friends need to know about addiction and recovery*

"*Soaring Above Co-Addiction* shares the author's experience of pursuing peace and happiness in the face of incredible turmoil. I was moved by the intensity of Lisa's situation and the strength she had to re-direct her mindset and shift her life direction toward success. The power of her intentions and the results she has achieved are remarkable. I believe that every person can use the tools and advice she shares to improve their personal relationships and gain additional self-belief and empowerment. Whether you have an addict in your life or not, I would highly recommend this book."

-Leah Bruns, President & Founder of "Puttin' on the Bliss"

Soaring Above Co-Addiction™

Helping Your Loved One Get Clean,
While Creating the Life of Your Dreams

Lisa Ann Espich

ISBN: 978-0-615-35975-5

Library of Congress Number
LCCN: 2010924330

cover illustration: istockphoto.com / chuwy
cover background photo: istockphoto.com / Jo-Hanna Wienert
cover and interior design: the RBDI group, LLC / Aimée Carbone

Published by
Twin Feather Publishing
PO Box 18910
Tucson, AZ 85731

This book is dedicated to my family:

To my husband, Dean—you've taught me my greatest lessons. My love for you is stronger than ever.

To my son, Jesse—I am so proud of your strength, your passion, and your artistic talent. You are the light of my life.

To my sister, Leah—thank you for being my best friend and personal cheerleader.

To my sister, Johannah—you are the most giving person I know. Your strength and perseverance is an inspiration.

To my mother—there are no words to properly express my gratitude for having you in my life. You've always lifted me, encouraged me, and shown me what true beauty is.

To my father—thank you for your unconditional love and for always being there when I needed you.

I love you all, and I am so thankful!

Note to Reader:

This book shares one family's journey from addiction to recovery. Throughout these pages you will find the ideas and beliefs belonging to the author—who is not a doctor, psychiatrist, or counselor. The intent of the author is to share her story of hope, and to offer information of a general nature to help readers in their quest for freedom from co-addiction.

Every situation involving addiction is unique. The reader should consult a qualified health-care professional for evaluation and advice. This book is not intended for, and should not be used in place of such care.

The author's goal is to inspire and to show each reader that recovery is possible. Her message: we all have the ability to soar!

Contents

Introduction

Being in a relationship with an addict is enough to drive the sanest person crazy. Your world becomes consumed with lies, uncertainty, and chaos. You lose your zest for life. Eventually you feel broken.

As much as you want the addict to get clean, you come to realize what a hopeless situation it can be. You stand by and watch as this person you love loses all sense of reality. They are lost, with seemingly little desire to find their way home. Your gut instinctively warns you that you should run away as far and as fast as you can.

Leaving, however, is many times easier said than done. You may not be financially prepared. You don't want to put your children through the stress of moving and changing schools. You're just too physically and emotionally exhausted to face divorce lawyers, court hearings, and all of the other inconveniences that surround leaving your spouse. You especially don't want to let go of your dream of a happy marriage.

As your loved one's addiction gets worse, you may start to isolate yourself in an attempt to avoid shame or embarrassment. There is a stigma attached to addiction, especially if it involves illegal drugs. With other illnesses, it is easier to accept support, and support is more easily given.

I

In our society, addicts are seen as bad people. Just look at how they are portrayed in movies and television, and it is clear what the perception is. They are considered immoral and degenerate. Friends who don't understand addiction and its effect on the family don't know how to offer help. Their advice is usually along the lines of, "You need to leave the bum." So families try to keep it a secret. The longer the secret is kept, the harder it is to be honest. So much time and energy gets invested in covering up the problems that it becomes harder and harder to reach out for help.

I am married to a recovering drug addict. For the first sixteen years of our marriage, my husband Dean was addicted to alcohol, crack cocaine, and prescription pills of all kinds. It caused years of devastation for our family. No matter how bad things got, though, the choice to leave always seemed impossible. I felt like I was in a prison even though there was nothing physically holding me there. In order to justify staying in an unhealthy relationship, I got really good at making excuses as to why I couldn't leave.

When my son Jesse was small I was a stay-at-home mom. My excuse at that time was money. How could I leave if I didn't have a job? Once I started working, I convinced myself that I was still not bringing in enough money to make it on my own. As the years went by, the excuses continued: Jesse's birthday is next month and I don't want to ruin his party; summer is coming up and we have that great vacation planned; school is getting ready to start and I don't want Jesse distracted; the holidays are coming up so I'd better wait until they're over.

Eventually, I was all out of excuses. My son was a healthy and confident teenager. I had worked my way up in my job and I was making a great income, more than enough to leave. There was nothing holding me back, yet I still felt stuck. I'm sure part of it was fear of the unknown. I wondered just how crazy my husband was due to his drug use. If I tried to leave, would it push him over the edge? Would we end up becoming the latest murder/suicide story on the evening news? Or would he become so lost in his drug use that one day I would pull up to a street corner and find him there: homeless, shriveled away to skin and bones, and begging for money? What would I say to my son sitting in the passenger seat next to me?

I had many fears about leaving, but I believe the main reason I stayed was because I loved my husband and I desperately wanted him to get well. I didn't want to give up on him as so many people thought I should. Eventually, though, I did reach a point when I was ready to leave him behind. I felt that I had given it my all and it was time to save myself. It was when I learned to let go and focus on my own life that positive changes started to happen, not only for me, but for my husband as well. The results were life-changing.

I write from the viewpoint of a woman who is married to a man with addiction; for this reason I choose to use the pronoun "him" throughout this book, but the message is for anybody (man or woman) in a relationship with an addict. Everyone's story is different, but the disease of addiction seems to cause the same pain, fear, and confusion, regardless of who you are. Some of what I share may sound like your own story. Some of it may sound foreign to you. My hope is that much of what I share will inspire you on your own path to happiness.

I look back and remember how helpless and alone I felt. I needed a friend who could understand my pain. Through these pages I would like to be that friend to you. I will share the changes I made that turned my life around. I am confident that anybody involved with an addict will gain from making these positive changes as well.

When you love somebody with addiction, it is easy to become consumed with trying to save him. His sobriety becomes your strongest desire. Sobriety is possible, and there are ways that you can help to speed it along. The process can still be painfully slow, though, and ultimately it is the choice of the addict.

You can start on your own recovery from the grip of addiction this very moment. You have the power to reinvent your life. Believe in yourself. You are stronger than any problems you face.

A Time for Change

When I found myself chasing a drug dealer through my neighborhood streets, I realized just how insane my life had become. I came home from work to find my husband, Dean, standing outside of his dealer's car. I knew it belonged to his dealer because I had seen the car before. I had followed my husband a couple of weeks prior when I had suspected that he was going to get drugs. The old white Cadillac parked outside my house was the same car I had seen that night. Coming home to discover my husband purchasing drugs right outside our home was more than I could stand.

As soon as I started to pull up into the driveway, the Cadillac sped off. I was too furious to let him get away that easily. I spun my car back around and took off after him. I knew it was crazy, but my anger had the best of me. I was tired of struggling to pay the bills while this lowlife took our money.

As he weaved in and out of the neighborhood streets, I stayed right behind him. He finally pulled over to the side of the road and stopped. I swerved my car up in front of his, blocking him from taking off again. My adrenaline had taken over and at that moment I felt invincible. I am not a big woman by any means. I am 5'3" and about 120 pounds, but that didn't keep me from walking right up to the side of his car to confront him.

His window was down, allowing me to get a good look at him. His dark black skin was shiny with perspiration, his head was shaved bald, and his impressively muscular arms were covered in tattoos. Normally I would be intimidated by somebody like this, but I felt no fear. I was surprised by my own aggressiveness.

"Don't you ever come around Dean or my home again, do you understand me?" I stated in the strongest voice I could force out.

"I don't know what you're talking about," he replied. As I looked into his eyes I could sense that he was nervous. I'm sure this was the first time he had ever had a crazed wife chase after him.

"Oh, I know who you are. You're the asshole who's been taking all of the money that I work so hard for. I have a son to worry about, and if I ever find out that my husband gives you another cent, you'll be sorry," I threatened.

"Look," he said with his hands up and his palms facing toward me. "I don't want any trouble from you. I don't know what you think is going on but you don't have to worry about me."

"I know exactly what's going on. I'm just warning you to stay away from my husband."

"Alright, no problem," he responded.

With that I turned around and got back into my car. As I pulled away, I pushed the gas petal to the floorboard, causing my tires to spin and kick gravel up at the Cadillac. For a brief moment I felt powerful. I was proud of myself for standing up to this seemingly tough man.

As I drove back home, I started thinking about how reckless my actions really were. I had no way of knowing what the outcome would be of a confrontation like that. I had no doubt that somebody who sells drugs would carry a gun on him. People get shot everyday when deals go bad. Here I was chasing after a drug dealer whom I had caught completely off guard.

At that moment I was able to look at myself clearly. I

realized that my life had spun out of control. Some say that addicts have to hit bottom before they will get help. Maybe the people involved with addicts have to hit a bottom as well. My life had become as crazy as my husband's. In many ways, even more so, because I was going through it all sober. I didn't have alcohol and drugs to help cover up the pain, and I didn't have an addiction as my excuse.

I was living a constant cycle of arguing and crying, driving around late at night looking for my husband, buying back our belongings from pawn shops, putting myself into dangerous situations, feeling alone and confused. Every attempt that I made to help my husband seemed to fail. Even the drug dealer I confronted sold more drugs to him just a few hours later. Something had to change.

That night I pulled out a journal that my sister had given to me as a gift. It was so beautiful that I could never bring myself to write in it. It had pictures of angels on the outside and its lined pages were trimmed in gold. I grabbed a pen and began to write.

I was able to find a lot of clarity through my writing. I remembered years back when I felt so confident. I had big dreams, but somewhere along the way I had given up on them. I wanted my husband to get well, but at the same time I knew that I had to start taking care of myself.

It had been so long since I put my own needs first that I could hardly figure out what those needs were. I created a detailed plan. It included exercise to improve my self-esteem, saving money for my future security, and putting a focus on my own emotional strength. I was ready to take my life back.

The next day I started to put my plan to work. I chose walking as my exercise. It didn't cost me anything and it got me out of the house. It felt good to be getting in touch with my body again. Years before I had been physically fit and I had forgotten how empowering exercise can be. Each evening after dinner I would change into my walking clothes and off I went.

That first week my husband was taken by surprise. "Where

are you walking to every night?" he had asked me in a worried tone. I think he feared that I had met up with some hunky neighbor and now we were having a passionate affair. I figured it might do him some good to worry about what I was up to for a change. After just one week of my new walking routine, I was already feeling stronger.

My next goal was to establish a savings account of my own. I set up an account through my work which came directly out of my paycheck. I started out small so my husband wouldn't notice. It wasn't long before I had several hundred dollars saved up. It was in my name, and for the first time in a long time I felt a little bit of security.

My pastime in the evenings became reading. My new friends were Dr. Wayne Dyer, Melody Beattie, and Depok Chopra, to name just a few. I looked forward to climbing into bed each night to take in their insight and knowledge. These authors helped to encourage me and with their advice I began to evolve.

I learned how to use affirmations and visualization, which helped me to become more positive. As the weeks passed, I was amazed at how much I had changed in such a short time. I was blooming into a new woman. Even though my husband was still caught up in his addiction, I was feeling peace within myself. For a long time I didn't think I could be happy if my husband wasn't clean, but I was now learning that my happiness wasn't about him at all.

My husband noticed the changes and I sensed a newfound respect from him. What was once a household filled with hostility had now become quite calm. Although he was still using, I was no longer consumed by his problems. I encouraged him to get professional help and he slowly became more receptive. But each time he got close to admitting himself into treatment, he would get scared and back out.

One day I woke up, looked around, and as if I suddenly had a new set of eyes, I realized that it was time to get out of this situation. I gave my husband an ultimatum. Either he went into treatment that day or I was leaving him. He had heard this threat before. I'm sure he thought I was bluffing, but this time I was ready to follow through. He chose not to go. The next morning I left with my son and moved into my father's home.

Leaving was the toughest thing I've ever done. Dean would show up at my father's doorstep wanting money, or wanting a shoulder to cry on, or threatening me (sometimes all three in the span of a few minutes). He was emotionally out of control and there were times when I feared what he might do. His addiction was testing me, but I stayed strong and refused to return home unless he went into treatment.

Close to one month later he was ready to surrender and get help. He admitted himself into a three month in-patient program. He emerged from treatment healthy and strong and with a new outlook on life. It has now been over five years, and we are sharing a healthy marriage together.

I now look back and see how quickly his recovery came once I left him to face his own reality. I have often thought about how much time had been wasted. If I had only stood up to his addiction a decade before, we might have avoided many years of turmoil.

But the truth is I just wasn't ready yet. I had, in fact, left him many times before, but I always quickly returned. It took building up my self-esteem and harnessing my inner strength in order to face that challenge. I know that Dean's courageous willingness to finally get help came as a direct result of my own personal changes.

I still occasionally catch myself falling into old patterns. I start to worry that Dean will lose his strength. I sometimes try to control situations, but I am healthy enough now to stop myself. Addiction is a cunning disease and could always rear its ugly head again. Relapse is many times a part of recovery. I know that Dean works every day to stay clean. I also know that my own positive outlook contributes to his success.

I used to look to my husband to make me happy. Because he was an addict, he always failed at that job. I now understand that I am in charge of my own happiness and that there is nobody in the world (including my own husband) who can steal it away from me.

We all want to believe that we will live to a ripe old age, but none of us knows our own fate. For those of us who love an addict, we tend to put off our own dreams and goals while we attempt to help our loved one get his or her life in order. We take the focus off our own lives in order to put all of our energy toward them. We may even come to believe that our sole purpose in life is to help save the addict.

Don't make the mistake of living your life in a supporting role. Our time here is fleeting. If you put your own desires aside, waiting for the right timing, your chance for personal fulfillment may come and go. This is your life—you're in the leading role. It's time to live it like the star that you are!

Suggestion:

I recommend keeping a journal as you make your way through this book. You may remember stories that you had forgotten about—write them down. Write any ideas that you read and want to remember. Write down your dreams and goals. Throughout this book, I will have more suggestions for your journaling. Keeping a record of your thoughts and feelings is an important part of this process. You don't need an expensive journal. A ninety-nine-cent spiral notebook is as good as anything. What your journal looks like is unimportant. It is the words that go into it that will have meaning.

Nobody gets to live life backward.
Look ahead, that is where your future lies.
-Ann Landers

I Take You, Dr. Jekyll...

Many of us grew up with the dream of "Happily Ever After". That was the fairy tale we were raised on. We believed that one day we would meet Prince Charming. As little girls, we may have planned our weddings and imagined how beautiful we would be as brides. We expected everything from there would just fall into place.

We're not always told about the realities of marriage and life; so when things get rocky, we believe that our lives are crumbling because we were not prepared. "Happily ever after" did not include missed mortgage payments, disagreeing on the type of discipline to use with the kids, and it certainly did not include sitting up all night worried that our missing spouse might be dead.

Loving a person who has a substance abuse problem is a lot like being in love with Dr. Jekyll and Mr. Hyde. On the one hand, there is this person that you fell in love with. He has all of those great qualities that you had always dreamed about finding in a man—great sense of humor, romantic, and caring. This is what keeps you around. You know that there is a wonderful man buried right under the surface.

Your friends and family just can't understand why you stay in a relationship with an addict. What they don't see is the incredible person he is when the timing is right—when he's clean for a few days and he hasn't become consumed with his cravings again yet. For a brief time, you have hope for a happy future. It's too bad that he has a villainous clone lurking inside of him. When his other personality is lured out by drugs or alcohol he becomes a man you hardly recognize.

Each addict takes on distinct characteristics when he's high. He may become very cocky and mean. Maybe he acts paranoid or takes on strange behaviors. The changes can be drastic. It really can seem like he's turned into a different person.

When my husband was using crack cocaine, everything about him was different: his voice, his personality, even his facial features seemed to change. He would act very similar to a person with mental illness. He would make strange twitches. He was paranoid. It was uncomfortable to be around him when he was high.

If I was home with him when he'd been using, I would be faced with his insane behavior. He would pace around the house like a caged animal, spending most of his time looking out the window. He was afraid of every car driving by and every little noise. He would typically find me and try to carry on some sort of conversation, attempting to act as if everything were normal.

He would ask me something like, "Did you feed the dog yet?"

"Yes, I fed the dog." I would respond, feeling annoyed. He would walk away, pace around the house, and stare out the window. And then, as if he were an eighty-year-old man with Alzheimer's disease, he would come back and ask me the same question again.

"Did you feed the dog yet?"

Frustrated that I just finished answering that question, I would ignore him. I would try to pretend he wasn't there. He would eventually walk away, pace around the house, stare out the window for a while, and then come back to where I was.

"Did you feed the dog yet?"

I would continue to ignore him and he would continue the same routine over and over again. Finally, after asking me the same question six or seven times, I would lose it.

"Yes, I fed the damn dog, okay? Isn't it obvious that I don't want to talk to you? I can't believe that I am married to such a freak." I would say the cruelest things when he was in this condition, but I was just so upset. He would stare at me with a confused look on his face, walk away, pace the house, stare out the window, and come back.

"Did you feed the dog yet?"

It was crazy! I would look at this person who acted nothing like the man that I married, and it was so pathetic. Why would anybody choose to be in that state? It just didn't make sense to me. I couldn't imagine any temporary feeling being worth the destruction that resulted from his using.

I had lost the man I loved. It was like having another woman come and steal him away. My husband never had an affair, but he did have a mistress. That mistress was his addiction, and in many ways, it was just like an affair.

While somebody having an affair may hide hotel bills and receipts for flowers and jewelry, I would find hidden pawn tickets and stashed paraphernalia. Instead of coming home smelling like perfume and having traces of lipstick on his collar, Dean would come home with the aroma of beer and the lingering smell of crack smoke on his clothing. There were mysterious phone calls from people I didn't know. He would disappear and I would not know where to find him. There were times when he would be gone the entire night.

I think facing an affair would have been easier than facing addiction. It would have made more sense anyway. I couldn't understand why my husband would choose the drug over his family—over his marriage. At least I could understand the attraction to another woman. The thing that always blew my mind is that he didn't even seem to enjoy the high. As soon as he would take a hit, he was a paranoid mess. Yet this was the thing that he was living for.

Dealing with any sort of disease is difficult. Nobody wants to watch a loved one go through an illness. But the disease of addiction has an especially dark side. It can tear a family apart. The side effects can be so cruel and hurtful that they can destroy the very love that exists. As a spouse, partner, or family member, how can you not take it personally when the addict is lying to you, stealing from you, and breaking promises? Unfortunately, these are the normal side effects.

To help you better understand what your loved one is up against, it's important to know what happens to the brain after chronic alcohol and drug use. Abusive drugs generate a large release of a chemical called dopamine into the brain. Our brain naturally releases this chemical when we are doing something that creates pleasure, such as eating chocolate or having great sex. This chemical is what produces that euphoric feeling. The amount of dopamine released by drugs is more concentrated and intense then the amount normally released by the brain.

As the drugs are used more and more, the brain gets used to receiving these large concentrations of dopamine so it reduces its own normal activity. The drugs also start to destroy the dopamine receptors in the brain. This makes it increasingly difficult to achieve the euphoric feeling. The addict eventually needs more of the drug in order to get high. It also becomes difficult to achieve any good feelings without the drug.

This is why you may see the addict in your life falling into depression. The things that created happy feelings for him in the past just don't do it for him anymore. The ordinary pleasures that most of us enjoy fail to stimulate the addict because he has gotten used to the intense high that drugs create for him. Because the brain stops creating that feeling of pleasure naturally, getting high becomes his one true desire.

The more he allows drugs to take over his life, the more out of control his life becomes. When he attempts to stay clean for any length of time, he is faced with the mess that he has created. This, combined with the inability to feel good, causes him to become obsessed with getting high again. He is overwhelmed by his problematic life and can see no way to fix it. A person with common sense would realize that getting high will just create more problems, but for the addict, the urge to feel pleasure (high) again becomes his only goal.

Continued drug use affects the same part of the brain that's used for reasoning and decision-making. So when you watch the addict in your life acting crazy, and you think he must have lost his mind, in many ways he has.

The good news is that the brain does have the ability to recover. There is a lot stacked up against our loved ones, though. Not only have their brains been affected, in most cases their lives have been turned upside down. Friendships have been destroyed. They've lost the trust and respect of their families and loved ones. They may have lost their jobs and many of their belongings. Their self-worth is at an all-time low. As they look up at the mountain of obstacles, they can become overwhelmed and give up.

When I first learned about the effects of drugs on the brain, it really scared me. I realized what a huge hurdle my husband was up against. At the same time, it gave me a new understanding that allowed me to stop taking the things he was doing so personally.

It would probably be impossible to ever reach a point where you're not affected by the things the addict does. Being lied to and betrayed is hurtful. But when you understand that the addict is not doing those things to purposefully hurt you, it can help in controlling your emotions. It really is a side effect of the disease.

This is not to say that you should ever put up with any type of abuse. Even if you had put up with verbal or physical abuse before, you must walk away from it now. When you walk away, you can do it in a loving way, without the emotional abuse that you yourself may have become accustomed to giving out.

Any words spoken in anger tend to be hurtful. Make it a point to limit any conversations when you are filled with this heated emotion. A simple statement such as, "I'm leaving now and I won't be back until we've both had time to calm down," easily becomes, "I hate you, you son of a bitch. I'm leaving and never coming back."

When you say things that you don't mean over and over out of anger, it takes the integrity away from your words. Just as you no longer trust your loved one with the promises he makes to you, he no longer believes in your words either.

While you can't control the addict and what he does, you can help to control the environment that he is in. If you are helping to create a positive environment when he is not using, this can help to encourage continued sobriety.

If your loved one doesn't use on any given day, then it is a day to be thankful. If you are doing your part to keep things peaceful, then you are encouraging sobriety. If there are no arguments, guilt trips, or shame involved, then he may see sobriety as something to work toward.

On the other hand, if his day is miserable, there will be no incentive for him to stay clean. Why would he choose sobriety if all it entails is dirty looks, screaming matches, and constant reminders of his failures? This is not to say that you can control how the addict's day goes. He can do a really good job of ruining the day all on his own. Your actions, however, can help to make the day worse or better.

As I started working on my own reactions toward my husband's drug use, I noticed huge improvements in the atmosphere of my home. It was no longer intolerable, and the constant arguing stopped. It is not easy to make these changes. Naturally you get upset when your loved one is using. Not acting out on that anger may feel like you're accepting the way things are. But ask yourself: has arguing with him ever worked before?

Try looking through the addict's eyes for a moment. Imagine waking up and making an attempt to start the day off on the right foot, but as soon as you cross paths with your spouse, you get a mouthful about how selfish and irresponsible you are. You accept these words because you know that you've earned them. So maybe you decide to do something nice like do the dishes, but your spouse is so angry that he or she just can't acknowledge the good deed. Your spouse may even make a negative comment such as, "It's about time you did something around here," leaving you feeling even worse about yourself.

As the day progresses, so do the cravings. You start to think about how difficult your life is. You convince yourself that staying clean for the day won't make any difference anyway. Once you start thinking about getting high, it's all over. You just need an excuse. You know that a good fight always does the trick. If you just say something to set off your spouse, you can have a really good reason to go out and get high. Your spouse is so emotionally sensitive that it takes no time at all for a huge argument to break out—victory.

The addict is a master manipulator. With your understanding of this, you can avoid falling prey to his traps. When he tries to start an argument, you can see it for what it is. You can walk away from his desperate attempts and avoid getting sucked in. He will be left with no excuse to use. If he decides to get high, he has only himself to blame.

As you start making these changes, it may feel uncomfortable. It might feel as though you're letting the addict get away with his behavior. You may have a lot of anger built up and you don't know how to release it. While it can temporarily feel good to let it all out in an argument, that release of toxic words is hurtful to the entire household. You may say things that you don't mean and the verbal abuse can have long-lasting effects.

You *can* find new ways of freeing negative emotions, which will leave you feeling good about yourself. Exercise or any physical activity is a great outlet. I've had some of my best workouts when I'm upset. If I feel like I'm ready to explode, I shut myself in my room, turn up the music, and work out my frustrations. When I'm done, my mind is cleared, my body is grateful, and I don't feel angry anymore. Writing in a journal is also an effective way to purge those emotions. Look for the activities that help you to feel better.

Your home should be your sanctuary. It should be your shelter from the craziness of the outside world. Sadly, in an addict household, it is the home that becomes the place of chaos. You can change that. Your own reactions will make the difference. You deserve peace and you can find that peace within yourself. Isn't it worth a try? What do you have to lose except anger, hostility, and craziness?

Journaling Suggestion:

Write about the two sides of the addict in your life. He may even have three or four sides. What brings these personalities to the surface and what are the warning signs that they are about to visit? Next, work out a plan of how you will react toward his negative side the next time you come face to face with it. Keep it positive, making sure to avoid any arguments. Leave enough space in your journal to come back and write about the outcome of your new approach.

To be happy, drop the words "if only" and substitute instead the words "next time."
-Smiley Blanton M.D.

A Familiar Story

Mary lifts the lid off the roasting pan, allowing the steam to escape, fogging up her glasses. She sticks a fork into the corner of the roast, tearing off a piece. She blows on it for a moment, then gently puts it into her mouth, pulling the meat off with her teeth. It is disappointingly dry. She puts the lid back on and glances at the clock.

Jim was supposed to be home an hour ago. She knows that if he doesn't get home soon, they won't make it to the movies on time. She picks up the phone and dials his cell phone number. It goes directly to his voice mail—never a good sign. *Why isn't he answering his phone,* she worries. She's come to hate the recording on his voicemail. All she hears when she gets that recording is, "Ha, ha, you can't get ahold of me." Frustrated, she hangs up without leaving a message.

She contemplates serving dinner to the kids now, but decides to hold out a few minutes longer. There's no way Jim would screw things up tonight, she convinces herself. He knows how much they've been looking forward to this evening all week. Robert and Sara have even gotten along all day.

With Robert being ten and Sara being six, it's difficult to keep the peace between them. She wishes her children were closer. Today was nice though. They watched videos together all afternoon without any arguments breaking out.

She looks at the clock again. Another fifteen minutes have gone by. The last couple of weeks, Jim has managed to stay clean and Mary has felt a sense of relief. Now all she feels is worry. *Please don't let him mess up tonight,* she prays. *Please don't let him disappoint the kids.*

She remembers the way things were when they first got married. She met Jim at law school and quickly fell in love. He was a year ahead of her and seemed so mature compared to the other guys that she had dated. As soon as Jim graduated and landed his first job at a law firm, he proposed to her. Once they were married, they started working on having a family and Mary put her career goals aside.

Several years into their marriage, Jim began drinking regularly and drugs soon followed. Before Mary knew it, she was married to a full-blown drug addict. He still had his weeks here and there when he would stay clean, and it was during those times she was hopeful that their family could be saved.

Jim finally pulls up into the driveway an hour and a half late. At first Mary feels a wave of relief, but then a knot forms in her stomach as she waits for him to walk in. Her instincts tell her that Jim will be high, but she holds out hope that her instincts are wrong. As soon as he steps in the doorway, she can smell the stench of beer. He doesn't want to look her in the eyes and he walks straight toward the bathroom.

"Where have you been?" Mary questions as she follows closely behind him.

He reaches the bathroom door and quickly shuts himself in. She wriggles the locked doorknob.

"Jim, where have you been?" she questions again. "Dinner has been ready for over an hour and we're all waiting for you."

"I'll be out it a minute," Jim replies in a voice that Mary has learned so well. She is able to tell now as soon as he says a few words if he has been doing drugs.

"I can't believe that you would do this tonight," Mary yells to him. "Now what am I supposed to tell the kids?" She lets out a groan of frustration as she walks to the kitchen.

She fills two plates with food as she fights back her tears. "Robert...Sara, dinner's ready," she calls out. They walk in slowly and sit at the table. As Mary sets their plates down, she looks at their sulking faces. It is obvious that they are already prepared for disappointment.

"Are we still going to the movie?" Robert asks.

"No, it looks like the movie is off," she answers.

Robert drops his fork down on to his plate. "I hate this family!" He screams, pushing his chair back and running from the kitchen.

Mary looks over at Sara. "I'm sorry, but it just didn't work out," she tells her. She sees the sadness in her daughter's eyes, but she is too upset herself to console Sara.

Mary walks back to the bathroom where her husband has locked himself in and starts pounding on the door.

"What in the hell are you doing in there?" she yells at him.

There is no reply.

"Jim, answer me, damn it! Come out here and stop being such an asshole!" She steps back and then kicks the door as hard as she can in an attempt to force it open.

"Stop it!" Mary hears her son scream. She turns around·to see Robert standing there, his face red with frustration, his eyes overflowing with tears. "Just stop it!" he screams again. She is immediately pulled back to reality. Robert turns and runs to his room, slamming his door shut. She looks down the hallway and sees her daughter standing there, her chest quickly moving in and out as she cries.

"Oh, Sara, honey, I'm sorry. Come here," she says, holding her arms out.

"No, I hate this family too!" Sara cries as she runs outside to the backyard. Mary knows that she should go after her daughter, but she just doesn't have it in her. She goes to her bedroom, shutting and locking the door. As she sits on her bed, the tears are too strong to hold back. *Please take me away from this,* she quietly prays. Crawling under the blankets, she wishes that the darkness could swallow her up.

Sara sits alone on the back porch. As the sun disappears, the air grows colder, causing her to shiver. Their sheepdog Barney walks over and she puts her little arms around him. She digs her face into his warm hairy neck and cries.

Robert lies on his bed staring at the ceiling. He had told his friends at school that he was going to see "Spiderman" tonight. What would he tell them on Monday morning? He plans in his mind how he is going to escape his crazy family. Within minutes of Jim coming home, the entire family has broken down.

Jim, who has been sitting in the bathroom, notices that the house has quieted. He splashes some water on his face and pulls himself together. As he opens the bathroom door he hopes that there is nobody there to face.

The house has grown dark. He goes to open his bedroom door but it's locked. He walks to his son's room and opens the door. Robert shoots him a nasty glare. Jim says nothing to his son as he closes the door behind him. He walks into the kitchen and sees the uneaten dinner still sitting there.

Jim really believed that he could grab a quick beer after work just to relax—nobody would know. But as soon as he finished his beer, he was overcome with his craving to get high. He just wasn't thinking clearly when he went to his dealer's house. He wasn't even thinking about the night that he had planned with his family.

He notices the back porch light on and sees his daughter outside. He goes to the sliding glass door that leads to the porch and gently knocks. Sara lifts her head up from her cozy spot on Barney's neck. "Come inside now," he calls. She gets up and walks into the house.

Jim can see from her puffy red eyes that she's been crying. He wishes he could say the right thing to make her feel better, but what can he possibly say? It's his fault that she's been crying. He's the one who ruined their plans.

"I'm sorry," he tells Sara. He retrieves his car keys from the pocket of his pants and walks out the front door. He gets into his car and starts driving back towards his dealer's house. He figures that there's no reason to fight his cravings since he has already destroyed the evening.

Mary had fallen asleep and is awakened by Jim knocking at the bedroom door to let him in. She glances at the clock and sees that it is 1:30 in the morning. She gets up and unlocks the door.

"Where have you been?"

"Just out," he answers as he pushes his way past her.

She can't believe that he would have an attitude toward her. She's the one who deserves to be mad. She pries her wedding band off of her finger and throws it at him. "I'm done. Do you hear me? Done. First thing tomorrow I'm taking the kids and leaving once and for all!"

"Stop yelling," Jim tells her. "You're going to wake up the kids. Just calm down and stop being so melodramatic."

"Melodramatic? How dare you? You have no idea what it's like to be married to a loser like you."

"Don't push it," Jim says, stepping towards Mary. She quickly backs out of the doorway and goes to the hallway bathroom, locking the door. She stands behind the door for a moment, waiting to see if Jim will follow her, but there is only silence. She turns and leans over the sink, looking into the mirror.

Mary's eyes are so swollen from crying that she can barely keep them open. *This has to end,* she tells herself. She puts the lid down on the toilet and sits. She tries to figure out a plan to leave her husband, but reality quickly hits. She's not working, they have no savings to speak of, and all of their credit cards are maxed out. How could she possibly make it on her own? Feeling defeated, she gets up and opens the bathroom door.

Looking down the hallway she sees that her bedroom door is shut. She leaves the bathroom and heads to her son's room.

She opens the door and peeks in. Robert is sound asleep. His TV is still on so she goes over to turn it off. She walks over and kisses his damp forehead. "Goodnight," she whispers.

She goes to Sara's room but finds her bed empty. Confused, she heads to the living room. Sara is there asleep on the couch. Mary walks over and slips a throw pillow under her daughter's head. Sara awakens and looks up at her mom. "Go back to sleep," Mary tells her daughter as she softly touches her cheek. Sara closes her eyes and rolls over onto her side.

As Mary stands over her daughter peacefully sleeping, she is overcome with guilt. She wonders what kind of mom leaves her kids all alone and locks herself in her room? It makes her feel terrible to think of them falling asleep without anyone even telling them goodnight.

She goes back to Sara's room and pulls the covers down on her bed, climbing in. Rubbing her finger where her wedding band was, she thinks about her kids and what all of this craziness must be doing to them. Her eyes burn so she closes them. Within moments she falls asleep.

The following day, the house is filled with tension. Mary is not speaking to Jim, which leaves the kids feeling uneasy. Robert asks if he can go to the park.

"Go ahead," Mary tells him. "Just take your sister with you." Surprisingly, he does not argue. They grab their bikes and head off.

Now that the kids are out of the house, Mary is free to speak her mind. She walks up to Jim, who has been sitting on the couch watching sports.

"Do you have any idea how badly you screwed things up last night?" she asks in a raised voice. "You obviously don't love me or the kids. Why don't you just take your stuff and get the hell out of our lives?"

Jim immediately turns the anger back on Mary. He didn't need her pulling this self-righteous stuff on him. If she wants a fight, she'll get a fight, he decides.

"Don't raise your voice at me!" he yells as he stands up from the couch. "I don't need this crap from you. You don't think I feel bad enough?" He swings at a can of soda that is sitting on the coffee table and sends it flying across the room. "You want me out of here? Well, I'm out of here." He grabs his car keys and leaves the house, slamming the door behind him.

As Jim drives away, he has no idea where he is going. He had been sitting on the couch trying to think of a way to make things up to his family. Trying to figure out what he could say or do to make things right again. Now all he can think about is getting high. He might as well. His wife has made it clear that she hates him. His kids probably hate him too. So he starts driving toward his dealer's house.

Mary wonders why she couldn't keep her mouth shut. She told Jim to leave, but it's actually the last thing she wanted him to do. Now she has no idea where he is going or when he'll be back. She picks up a framed wedding photo that is sitting on the fireplace mantel. Letting out a scream she throws it as hard as she can across the room. It hits the wall, causing the glass to smash into pieces. She drops to the floor as she begins to cry uncontrollably. She feels like she is going crazy.

This is a typical scenario in an addict household. It is based on a story that was shared with me while I was preparing this book. The woman sharing her story was obviously still distraught even though several days had passed since this incident. She cried as she spoke, and it was clear from her words that she was filled with resentment. I sympathized with her because I have been through similar circumstances of my own. Does any of it sound familiar to you?

There is the spouse who feels helpless over her circumstances. She wants to be a good mom, but finds herself handling situations badly because her own emotions are so out of control. There are the children who truly have no power over what is happening in their household; they are the real victims here.

Then, of course, there is the addict who seems to be the villain. In reality he is filled with guilt and shame over the hurt that he has caused, but that does not keep him from using. In fact, the worse he feels, the more he craves. The more he gets high, the more problematic his life becomes, which in turn makes him want to use even more. It's a vicious cycle.

As I listened to her story, I couldn't help but think how differently this whole situation could have turned out if she had just handled herself differently. It's easy to see that when you are on the outside. Imagine how different this scenario could have been if Mary had taken better control over her own actions that night.

When Jim came home high, Mary reacted as if all of their plans had been destroyed. But Jim is only one member of this family. Mary gave him complete control over the outcome of the evening. If she had sat down and enjoyed dinner with her two children, the rest of the night could have turned out so much better. Jim not being there would certainly have been a disappointment, but there was no reason to ruin the night for everyone.

If the family had left and gone to the movies without Jim, he would have been given an opportunity to really think about his actions. It can be scary for an addict to realize that the people close to him are going on with their lives. He would have probably been surprised that they would go have fun without him. *Maybe they don't need me after all,* he may have thought to himself. At the same time, he would not be taking on the extra guilt of knowing that he ruined the evening for his wife and kids—and that's a good thing. The more guilt that addicts are left with, the more they crave getting high or drunk in order to cover up those feelings.

On the other hand, maybe nothing would have been different for Jim. He might have made another trip to his dealer's house regardless of what Mary and the kids did. It surely would have been a better night for the rest of the family though. They would have enjoyed their dinner. They would have had fun together at the movies. There would have been no crying or arguing going on.

You deserve to be living a happy and positive life. If you are spending a lot of your time feeling angry and resentful, you are far from living positively. You may have a hard time letting go of that anger. You may feel that you've earned the right to be angry. Besides, you want life to be miserable for the addict every time he gets high because it might convince him to finally stop.

When your loved one comes back down from getting high or drunk, do you take that as your opportunity to tell him how wrong he has been? What a terrible husband and father he is? That he doesn't deserve you? Do you argue and cry? Is this working for you yet?

All of these things that you tell him, he already knows. You may not realize it, but the addict is usually harder on himself then anybody around him. There really is no need to remind him over and over again. He knows exactly what he has done.

It's important to realize that you cannot control his actions. He is going to do what he wants to do whenever he wants to do it. Have you ever tried to stop him from using once his mind is made up? Did you succeed? My guess is that you may have stalled him for a few hours at the most, but eventually he got what he was after. Once the addict has made up his mind to get high, there is usually no stopping him.

One of the definitions of insanity is doing the same thing over and over again and expecting a different outcome. Do you find yourself acting insane? Do you react the same way toward your loved one every time he gets high, expecting it to make a difference even though it has never worked before? Although you can not control what he does, you can learn new ways to interact which can have a positive impact.

The best thing that you can do is to start focusing on yourself. When you stop trying to control him, and put your attention on your own actions, real change will start. In an addict household it is easy to get stuck in a pattern. Time and time again you play out the same old scenes; you make the same threats, he makes the same promises, and you have the same arguments.

I encourage you to make a vow to break out of that mold. The ideas shared in this book will help to empower you to make those changes. The new path you create for yourself will invite your loved ones to follow—even the addict. It's time to start a new chapter in your life. I hope it proves to be your best chapter so far.

Journaling Suggestion:

Write about the last argument that you and your loved one had. Try to remember every detail. Did you say the same things that you always say during arguments with him? Did you make threats that you knew you wouldn't follow through on? What are the negative patterns in your home? Are you constantly threatening divorce? Do you say hurtful things in front of the children that leave you feeling terrible later? Those are the things that you want to be aware of. While you can't control what the addict says or does, you can begin to change your own negative patterns.

> **Happiness is not the absence of conflict,**
> **but the ability to cope with it.**
> -Anon

Letting Go

You *can* detach from the problems of addiction. Yes, you are in a relationship with an addict, but in order to love him, you do not need to stay down in the storm with him. You can rise above the dark clouds. You can serve as an example of health and happiness. Not only is it possible, but it is the best thing that you can do for yourself and for the addict.

It may seem like an impossibility to separate yourself from such a difficult situation. You may convince yourself that it would be irresponsible—that if you're not right there in the middle to attempt to salvage what's left of your loved one's job, his reputation, and his self-respect, that everything will just crumble around both of you and be destroyed.

Here's the tough reality—things need to start crumbling around him in order for him to realize his need for help. I know that you believe that you're doing the right thing when you help him to save his job, or help him to stay out of jail, or save him from whatever horrific thing is getting ready to happen. But it's not helping him, it's helping his addiction. You're making it easy for him to continue drinking or using, because the consequences aren't bad enough to convince him to stop.

Think about how much you despise the addiction. It's like

an evil demon that has taken over your loved one's body. You claim that you're willing to do anything that you can to get rid of it. Instead you become an accomplice to it.

Having spent time listening to other people share their stories in family recovery meetings, I have noticed a common thread amongst us spouses. As our loved ones progress in their disease, we fall into our own downward spirals. We manipulate situations in an attempt to control the outcome. We learn to avoid functions because of our fear of embarrassment. We find ourselves lying on a regular basis to friends, family members, judges, probation officers, and, sadly, to ourselves.

Because we can no longer rely on our husbands, we gradually take over all of their manly and fatherly duties. We change the oil in the car, mow the lawn, build the new deck, teach our sons to play catch. We may even become the sole breadwinner of the household. Meanwhile, we leave our husbands responsible for nothing—all out of the hope that we can somehow control our crazy circumstances—that we can somehow hold our marriage and family together all on our own. It's no wonder that we grow resentful.

It is a difficult thing to let go and allow him to face the consequences of his actions, mostly because it affects your well-being as much as his. You don't want your life to become more stressful. You don't want your husband to lose his job and leave you broke. You don't want to admit to your family and friends how bad things have gotten. So you do everything in your power to keep the outside world from finding out.

When it comes to the other people in our lives, especially the addict, we must learn to let go. We can't make their choices for them. We can't control what they do and the more we try, the more out of control our own lives become.

Here is a quick visioning exercise that can help when you are having a difficult time letting go. I first experienced using this visualization when listening to Susan Jeffers, Ph.D., author of *Feel the Fear and Do It Anyway*™ in the audio program, *Empowering women* (Hay House). I've made a few changes, but this exercise has helped me to let go on many occasions. Read through it first and then try it with your eyes closed.

Imagine that the addict is standing right in front of you. Notice that there is a thick cord that ties the two of you together. Every time he moves he pulls you with him. If you try to move in the opposite direction, he overpowers you, making it too difficult. So, here you are being forced around wherever he chooses to take you. The more you resist the tighter the cord gets, causing you to feel suffocated. You are left with two choices. You can surrender and become his prisoner or you can cut the cord and let him go. Imagine pulling out a large pair of scissors. Now, cleanly and swiftly, cut the cord. As soon as you do, you feel a release. You are no longer constricted. You are free.

This is a great exercise to try anytime that you are feeling caught up in the addict's world. You may find that there are times when it seems impossible to mentally cut the ties, but the more you practice letting go, the thinner and weaker the cord between you will become. When an argument starts to break out, or at times when you are feeling resistance, you can quickly imagine cutting that cord, and simply walk away.

Detachment is really about doing what you can to distance yourself from the troubles of addiction. It is about letting the addict deal with the consequences of his actions. You can begin to detach immediately. It does not mean that you have to make the decision to pack your things and move out—maybe you will never need to leave. But by putting a stop to enabling behavior, you can improve the odds for positive change.

There are many examples of enabling that happen in an addict household. I offer the following scenarios as examples of how enabling behavior happened in my own home, and the changes I made. You know your situation better than anybody, and only you can decide what changes are safe to make.

I personally reached a point, that if Dean passed out on the bathroom floor, I left him there. What would have happened if I spent half of my evening trying to get him up and into bed? Not only would I have lost out on my own well-needed rest, but when he woke up, it's likely he wouldn't have remembered passing out on the floor in the first place. My stories of hauling him to bed, and cleaning up vomit off of the bathroom floor, would have just sounded like exaggerated whining to him.

Instead, by leaving him there and going to bed on my own, I woke up refreshed, and he woke up on a cold hard floor with a stiff neck and a dose of reality. I decided that enough mornings like that, and he might start to wonder if his addiction was getting the best of him.

My husband used to have a nasty habit of kicking our kitchen garbage across the floor when he had been drinking and was upset about something. He did this on more than a few occasions. We would be arguing about his drinking and he would give the garbage can a full-blown kick, causing the disgusting contents to fly all across the kitchen. After that he would take off, leaving his mess behind. I would then spend the next hour cleaning it up so that the reminder of his tantrum was completely gone by the time he came back home. How silly of me. What possible reason did he have to stop doing this?

So one night he did it again, but I didn't lay a finger to clean it up. I wasn't sure how he would react, but I knew that I was done with this ridiculous game. I was asleep by the time he got back. When I woke up the next morning, the kitchen was clean, and it never happened again.

If Dean didn't get up to go to work because he got too wasted the night before, I did not call his work for him. Of course, I don't think I could have followed through on this boundary if I wasn't working myself. If he had ended up losing his job, and I had no income coming in, where would that have left our finances? This is why it is so important to get some financial independence of your own. The dynamics of a relationship when only one partner has an income can be difficult for even the healthiest of marriages. When you mix in your husband's addiction problems, it can leave you in a vulnerable position.

Many times financial burden is what keeps us bound to our current circumstances. Most of us can't afford to walk away from our homes and jobs in order to start a new life. I believe that this is one reason why celebrities tend to end their marriages so quickly. It is not that they are less committed than the rest of us, but rather that they are making high-dollar paychecks. When they find themselves in the middle of an unhealthy relationship, they have the means to get up and leave.

While most of us may never have millions of dollars in the bank, we are all capable of our own financial independence. As you make your way toward that goal you will no longer feel like a prisoner.

I was home for eight years with my son, and although I would never give that time back, I know that it kept me mentally and physically stuck. I had no income of my own to fall back on so I put up with a lot more than I probably would have if I had had my own paycheck coming in. The mistake I made was in believing that I could not be at home with my son and make an income at the same time. But making your own money does not necessarily mean that you have to find a job outside of your home. Consider the benefits of a home-based business.

There are so many options and literally hundreds of books and online resources available that can help you to get started on the right path. Start by asking yourself, what are you good at? I would bet, whatever it is, there is a way to make money at it. Here are some ideas to get you thinking:

Avon Representative	Bookkeeper
Cake Decorator	Caterer
Childcare Provider	Cleaning Service
Computer Trainer	Dog Trainer
Event Planner	Fitness Trainer
Freelance Writer	Gardening Consultant
Hairstylist	Home Healthcare
House Sitter	Jewelry Designer
Laundry Service	Manicurist

Mary Kay Representative	Massage Therapist
Music Instructor	Pet Groomer
Pet Sitter	Photographer
Professional Organizer	Resume Service
Seamstress	Website Developer

These are just a handful of the hundreds of home-based businesses that you can start up. Some of them require certificates or special schooling—some don't. Many of them entail almost no start up costs. The opportunities that exist are vast. Self-employment allows you to control the hours you work and the tax write-offs are incredible.

Maybe starting a business is not for you. What do you see in your future? Is there a career that you have always dreamed of having? Would you like to go back to school to pursue that dream? Even if you just take one class at a time, it is a step in the right direction. If you think you can't afford it, contact your local community college. You might be surprised by the financial support that is available.

If you are already working for a company, then you should be looking at the opportunities that they offer. Many times just letting your supervisors know that you are interested in moving ahead will open their eyes to your potential. If you are working for a company that offers you no hope for advancement, then you may want to look at other options for employment.

As you start to focus on your future, be sure to learn as much about finances as you can. Be smart with your money. This can be challenging with an addicted partner, but there are ways to keep your money out of harm's way. For example, you can set up a savings account that takes the money directly out of your paycheck. The harder it is to get to the money, the better.

Read books by financial experts such as Susie Orman. It doesn't matter if you only have twenty dollars in the bank. The more informed you are, the more empowered you become. *Do What You Love; the Money Will Follow,* by Marsha Sinetar, is a terrific book, especially on tape. Marsha is very compassionate and wise. *The Automatic Millionaire*, by David Bach, teaches you how easily you can start to build wealth through simple changes. For example, you can buy an espresso machine and make your special morning coffee at home, instead of purchasing that five dollar Grande Mocha Latte every day.

In one year, five dollars a day adds up to $1825.00. Now imagine if you found a couple more opportunities and you turned five dollars into fifteen dollars. At the end of the year you would have $5475.00—and that's without any interest. It may be hard to give up little splurges, but as the money starts to grow, you will appreciate the security it provides far more than some temporary pleasures.

You deserve special treats, and I am not suggesting that you give them up, but how can you shave down on their costs so that you can start saving that extra money for yourself? If you've structured your relationship in a way that has left you a financial prisoner, you must start looking for opportunities to free yourself from that trap.

If you don't have your own career or source of income, then now is the time to start thinking about your future. You cannot count on an addicted partner to support you financially. You have no control over the choices that he will make and, unfortunately, those choices could leave him jobless or in jail.

As your loved one witnesses the changes in you, it will frighten him. The addict in him will desperately look for ways to pull you back in. His addiction may worsen. He may fall into depression, leaving you very concerned. Just know that this is his addiction attempting to con you and draw you back in. When you find your emotions falling back into anger or sadness, it is a warning that you are entering the storm of addiction. You can make a conscious decision to stay back.

As you move in this new direction, you will find yourself growing more and more confident. You are putting your focus back where it belongs—on you. You may find that you are not so emotionally attached to the addict anymore. You learn to allow him to make his own choices and to face his own consequences.

It can help to remember that with each mistake he makes, he is one step closer to realizing his need for help.

In the meantime, you start making healthy choices for yourself. You are setting a good example, not only for him, but for your children as well. You are focusing on your positive future (with or without him). You are getting strong and that is the real goal of detachment.

Journaling Suggestion:

Write about the different ways that you have helped to enable your loved one's addiction. Do you make excuses for him? Lie for him? Have you taken over many of his responsibilities? What might have happened if you hadn't done these things for him? Would he have lost his job? Lost his driver's license? Ended up in jail? If you can learn to let the crisis happen for him, it might just save his life. The consequences could be bad enough to scare him into recovery. Most importantly, as you learn to let go of his problems, you are taking steps toward your own mental health.

There is just one life for each of us: Our own.
-Euripides

You Are In Control

You are the only one in control of your life. It may not feel like it at times. You may believe that your circumstances are controlling how you live and how you feel, but you are not a spectator watching your life unfold by the sidelines. You were born with free will. You are offered endless options every day and you make the choices.

It's easy to fall into the trap of believing that you are the victim. I would be so happy, you tell yourself, if he would just get clean. If it wasn't for my loved one's addiction, I would have the job of my dreams, but how can I go out and get a new job when I have to worry about him? If my husband wasn't spending all of our money on drugs and alcohol, we would have enough to buy a home of our own. I wouldn't be so depressed all of the time if I didn't have an addict ruining my life. You can go on and on.

There is no denying how difficult it is to love somebody with an addiction problem. Many people would agree that you have the right to feel depressed. The question to ask yourself is whether or not you want to feel that way. Holding on to hurt feelings is a choice that we make. Things happen around us that affect our lives. We cannot control these outside forces. We can, however, control our reactions to them.

When the addict comes home high or drunk, *you* make the choice of how to react. You can allow your blood to boil, tell him what a useless bum he is, argue and cry, and spend the rest of the evening feeling sorry for yourself. Or, on the other hand, you could look at him in his true light and remind yourself that he is sick. You could choose to see his problem as his and not yours. Make a conscious decision not to react. Then the important thing is to walk away. If you know that you will have to leave the house in order to have some peace, then leave the house. Just don't allow yourself to get caught up in the same old junk.

When he is in bad shape, what he really wants is the attention. He knows inside that he is weak, so having control over your reactions helps him to feel powerful, and if you're so angry then you must really care about him. He's used to you reacting a certain way.

He goes out and gets wasted. He then comes home to your threats and tantrums, but he knows that eventually you will calm down. He can then apologize and tell you how this was the last time. He loves you and will never do it again. He might even start crying. He knows just the right things to say because he has had a lot of practice figuring out what you want to hear. It's a routine that both of you have gotten used to. You know that when he says it won't happen again, it's an empty promise, but you want so badly to believe it.

Now, what if you made a different choice when he walked in the door? What if this time you made a comment to him such as, "I'm sorry you're not having a good day. I'll be back later when you're not high anymore." And then leave. How do you think he might react to that?

Chances are he wouldn't know what to do with himself without you there. This isn't the norm. He's used to the arguments. He might even use them as an excuse to drink or use more.

Then what do you do? You look for an activity to help you feel better. This would be a perfect time to visit an Al-Anon meeting. How about a relaxing long walk? Do you have a close friend that you can visit? Maybe there is a good movie playing.

There are so many things that you can do to enjoy your time and to get your mind off your loved one's problems. The point here is to stop living your life around what he is doing. I did just that for so many years. When my husband was clean, life was good. When he was high or in a bad mood, life was miserable. His highs and lows were always extreme and I was right there following his lead.

Maybe you have small children or a baby at home. This is even more reason to stay composed. It is not fair to your children for you to lose control of your emotions. They need to feel safe. Unfortunately, you can't hide your spouse's condition, and your children, no matter how small, will see that their dad is not acting normal.

Make sure to keep things as calm in your home as possible. If you know that you will not be able to avoid an argument, then the only right thing to do is to leave with your kids. Is there a park near your home that you can take them to? The library is a great place to hang out. You might need to spend the evening at a family member's home. Be prepared for these times.

When my husband was caught up in his addiction, I always kept an overnight bag in the trunk of my car just in case I felt the need for a quick escape. In my bag was a change of clothes and pajamas for both my son and me, a couple of toothbrushes, and travel size toiletries. That way, if I wanted to leave, there weren't any dramatic productions of me packing up my things to go. If, an hour after leaving, I changed my mind and wanted to come back home, he never had to know that I was packed to leave.

The toughest habit for me to break was the threatening. The urge to tell him that I was leaving him for good, that I was divorcing him, that he was going to regret not having me in his life. I wanted him to be frightened so that he would change his ways, but threats don't work—at least not long-term.

Sure, he got worried the first couple of times that I threatened leaving, but after my repeated failure to follow through, he caught on. He knew that I was just blowing off steam and eventually my threats didn't concern him much anymore.

I remember one Saturday afternoon when Dean came home drunk after watching a football game with some friends. We had plans for the evening, so I went out of control with anger when he stumbled through the door. Well, I was going to show him! I took my son and left. I rented a hotel room with the intention of staying away for the night so that he could spend the evening worrying about where I was for a change.

Within an hour of checking into the hotel, I was already feeling anxious. What if he was out looking for me? I didn't want to be responsible for him drinking and driving. A few more hours went by and I became more and more stressed. What if he was worried that we got into an accident? This was the first time that I had ever left without telling him where I was going. I did have his son, after all. He had a right to know where we were.

I tried calling home but there was no answer. I was concerned that he might have the entire family out looking for us by then. After being gone about six hours, I finally decided to go back home. When I got there, I found Dean passed out on the couch in the same position that he was in when I first left. While I had spent my entire afternoon worried and stressed, he was oblivious to the fact that I was ever gone.

If you decide to leave your home for an hour, or the evening, or even for a week, do it for yourself. Do it because you need the peace and quiet, because you want to take care of yourself, because you need the time to reflect and figure out what's best for you. But don't do it to manipulate. If you make threats that you don't truly mean, or leave with the intention of scaring the addict into recovery without being prepared to really stay away until he enters treatment, then your threats will only backfire on you.

Even if you never have to utilize it, it's a good idea to have a plan. Life is unpredictable when you are living with an addict. Learn to walk away from arguments or violence. Sometimes the only way to do that is to leave your home. If and when you decide to come back, only do so once you feel peaceful and you're confident that your situation is safe.

Maybe you're thinking that this just isn't fair. Why should you have to leave your home during these times? You're not the one with the problem. You should be kicking him out until he's cleaned up enough to come back. Well, you're right. It isn't fair. But you are making the choice every day whether or not to leave your situation.

You know that you're with an addict, so these times are going to happen. If you don't want to face them, then you have the options of moving out or kicking him out. You have the choice of staying married or getting a divorce. You are making the decisions every step of the way. If you decide not to leave, then you have to decide how you are going to react when your loved one is under the influence, because it inevitably is going to happen.

Every day, at every moment, you are making the decisions that lead you to the next step in your life. If you do not feel that the path you are taking is right for you, then you need to make the choice to get off that path. You have to intentionally turn yourself in a different direction and start moving that way. This can be petrifying, and it is why so many people stay stuck in a lifestyle that they are unhappy with.

You know that you want to make a change, but you're unsure of the right steps to take. What if you make a wrong choice? What if you end up worse off than before? There are no guarantees, and sometimes it feels safer to stay put. Just know that you decide for yourself.

In the twelve-step program, AA, they have the saying, "One day at a time." You can adopt this motto as well. During times of stress you can become overwhelmed, but the only question you need to ask is, *"What can I do today to be safe and peaceful?"*

Listen inside for the answer. There may be times when you need to take it one hour at a time, or even one minute at a time. Your top priority should always be the safety of yourself and your children.

When you're involved with an addict, you get used to living reactively. You're constantly waiting for the next big crisis. You have a difficult time enjoying the good times because you don't believe that they'll last. It's like driving with a blindfold on. You don't know what to expect from one moment to the next. You just hang on and hope that you survive.

You can make the choice to live proactively instead. You can keep your eyes wide open and take control of the steering wheel. When you live proactively, you have a plan and a roadmap. There may be detours, but at least you know the direction you're heading.

So how do you find this map? You create it. You do some soul-searching to figure out what you want and where you want to go. It's a lot like planning a trip. Your needs will depend on your destination. Your options are endless. Only you know what your truest desires are.

Don't limit yourself because of circumstances, financial status, age, or education. The only thing holding you back from achieving your dreams is your own beliefs. Every new day is a chance for a fresh start. Let go of the fear, anger, and resentment that are keeping you bound. The quickest way to free these emotions is through forgiveness.

Forgiveness is not about letting people off the hook. You don't have to forget about what has happened. You can learn the lessons available and grow stronger. You can start to set boundaries and hold to them. Forgiveness is letting go of the anger inside your own heart—letting yourself move past the pain so that it does not hold you back and keep you stuck.

When you are hurt by somebody, you might try to hang on to that pain. You don't want to let it go because you want to show that person how much you're suffering. You want them to feel as badly as you do. The hurt turns to anger. After time, the anger turns to resentment. You are then walking around consumed by all of these horrible feelings. You are allowing an outside force to dictate how you feel inside your own skin. By holding on and not forgiving, you are only hurting yourself.

The more that you learn about and understand addiction, the easier it becomes to forgive. It's sad to think of what a prisoner an addict really is. To not have control over one's own actions must be frightening. The guilt that gets carried around due to those actions must be overwhelming. They are hurting themselves far more than anybody else around them. Seeing them from empathetic eyes rather than angry eyes can help you to forgive.

Just as it is important to have forgiveness for other people, it is especially important to have forgiveness for yourself. So you have not always made the right choices. Who has? Maybe you get mad at your husband and scream at him in front of the kids—forgive yourself. You get down in the dumps and eat a whole gallon of rocky road ice cream—forgive yourself. You made an internal promise that you wouldn't spend the evening crying the next time your husband comes home drunk, but that's exactly what you end up doing—forgive yourself. You are in a bad situation and you have every right to do all of those things. Forgive yourself, and decide that the next time around, you will handle your situation in a healthier way.

When you notice that your emotions are getting out of whack, try to catch yourself. Stop and remind yourself that you are in control. Then make a decision as to what the next step is from there. If it's shutting yourself in the bathroom to take a long steaming hot bath, then that's what you do. If it's grabbing the kids and going to get pizza, then that's what you do. Start asking yourself what you would want to be doing right now if you weren't dealing with this addiction problem—and then do it anyway.

For a long time, I walked around with a knot in my stomach that would never go away. Like a lot of people, I hold my anxiety in my gut. When I am upset or worried about a situation, I can feel that tension right there in the pit of my stomach. I've found that a quick fix to relieving a lot of that tension is simply to focus on my breathing. I stop and slowly take in five to ten deep breaths. As I exhale, I imagine all of that anxiety exiting out and blowing away. It seems like such a simple exercise, yet it really helps.

I started using this exercise to reverse the problems that I was having with my stomach and to calm myself down when I was getting emotional. When my husband would come home high or drunk, instead of letting my emotions get all bent out of shape, I would step aside and do my breathing exercise. Within moments I would feel better. This allowed me to handle the situation in a much healthier way. Instead of spending the evening arguing, I would go on with whatever I wanted to do without him. As I got better at controlling my emotions, the knot in my stomach began to go away.

Don't get me wrong—I still would get down in the dumps. I definitely still had my emotional outbursts. Eventually, though, they became shorter outbursts. I came to realize that it just felt better to let go of the anger and give myself permission to enjoy my life.

Are you walking around with a hard knot in your stomach all the time? Are you ready to start feeling good? I guarantee that if you take control of your own emotions and start pulling yourself away from the chaos, you will feel better. One day soon, you might wake up and realize that the knot has gone away.

Journaling Suggestion:

Write about the different ways that you have felt victimized by your loved one's addiction. Are there goals that you have put off? Friendships you have lost? Are you struggling financially? Do you feel depressed much of the time? Are you sick, overweight, or worn down? Write about all of those negative circumstances in your life that you have blamed on the addict. Then go back and take a closer look. Be open to accepting responsibility. For each area that you wrote about, come up with a way that you can make a positive change, regardless of your loved one's actions. For example: if you wrote that you no longer go out with friends because the addict embarrasses you when he drinks, make a lunch date with just the girls. Then, most importantly, follow through on your plans.

The tragedy is not that things are broken.
The tragedy is that they are not mended again.
-Anon

Taking Care of You

As I write this, I am sitting on a cushioned lounge chair in a blue and white-striped cabana. It overlooks a salt water pool nestled in the middle of the Arizona mountains. I am enjoying the monthly retreat that my twin sister Leah and I share together. For the day, we escape to one of the many resorts that surround the Tucson area. We pack up some good books, writing material, and our bathing suits. We spend the day relaxing and enjoying each other's company.

This might seem like an expensive luxury, but it is actually quite reasonable. For the price of one treatment (we usually pick a massage), we have access to all of the resort's facilities. We can work out in the state-of-the-art weight rooms, enjoy the pool and Jacuzzi areas, and lounge around in big comfy white robes.

Special treats like this are a part of my new lifestyle. I used to believe that pampering this way was selfish. I would overhear women talk about the massage they got, or show off their new manicures, and I would think how self-involved they must be. Think of what they could be spending that money on instead, such as extra groceries, new plants for the patio, or art supplies for the kids.

I couldn't imagine spending money on myself like that. It

was just not in my makeup at the time. I actually took pride in how low-maintenance I was. I would remind my husband that he was lucky to have a wife who cut her own hair and didn't bother to grow her fingernails.

It is one thing to be smart with money, but it is something else altogether to deny ourselves little luxuries simply to stay in a martyr mentality. I believed it gave me some sort of power to remind my husband how much of our money he spent on liquor and drugs while I was clipping coupons and bargain shopping to save us money. I was the selfless saint whom he was fortunate to have in his life. In reality, all I was doing was giving him more money to spend on his habits. If I had treated myself to a massage or a new outfit once a month, the worst that would have happened is he would have had to skip getting high once or twice.

Most women, from the time they were little girls, were raised to be caretakers. We learned early on that we should be sweet, play nice, and put others first. While the boys around us were playing cops and robbers, we were busy playing house. We were taking care of our dolls and cooking dinner for our imaginary husbands. It is no surprise that we then grow up feeling like we have to put everybody's needs before our own.

It usually takes two incomes to survive financially these days. Yet, when you talk to women who are working full-time, they will usually tell you that they are pulling double duty. While their husbands come home ready to relax for the evening, the women are coming home to start their second shift. Dinner has to be made, dishes washed, homework checked, and laundry for the next day needs to get done. When you're married to an addict, you have the extra stress of trying to keep peace in a crazy household.

As women, what are we teaching our children? We must realize that we can't be good role models if we can't learn to take care of ourselves. We want our daughters to learn to have self-respect, and we want our sons to learn to treat women well. This starts with the examples that we set.

We may expect that our angelic qualities will eventually pay off for us. We wait for that special day to come when everybody treats us like a queen for being such a giving mom and wife. Then we become bitter as time goes by and that day never comes.

When my son was small, I used to take him to the library every week. One of the books on the suggested reading list was *The Giving Tree,* a short story written by Shel Silverstein. It was written in 1964, but is still popular today. I checked out the book, and that night we climbed into bed to read the story.

It was about the relationship between a little boy and a tree. The boy would eat the tree's apples and swing from her branches, which made the tree happy. But as the boy grew older, he wanted more and more from the tree. In order to make the boy happy, the tree ends up giving the boy all of her apples to sell, all of her branches to build a house, and eventually her trunk to build a boat to sail away. As long as the boy was happy, then the tree was happy too.

At the end of the story, the boy, now an old man, returns to the tree who has nothing left but her stump. She feels bad because she has nothing left to give. She ends up offering her stump for the old man to sit on, which in turn makes her happy.

When I finished reading the story I remember thinking, *that is one codependent tree.* I was unsure of the message intended. Was the author trying to teach our children that this is what love is all about?

While I did not find it to be a good example of love or of giving, the story stuck with me, and I do think that it has a great lesson attached to it—*if you give and give of yourself without ever asking for or expecting anything in return, eventually you will be nothing but a dead old stump.*

As women we deserve to be pampered. You don't have to wait for an outside source to give you what you deserve. When you start treating yourself as special, you will then be teaching the other people in your life how to treat you. This doesn't mean that you are supposed to become a self-centered prima donna. But you will find that when you start giving yourself the attention you deserve, your self-esteem flourishes.

What do you consider pampering? Have you always dreamed of being treated to a hot rock massage? Is the idea of having your own personal trainer appealing to you? Is enjoying brunch with close friends in an outdoor café more your style? If you could enjoy pampering in any way that you desire, what would it be?

Now what's stopping you? Is it money? If so, then it's time to start your own pampering fund. Every chance you get, keep adding to your fund until there's enough money to treat yourself. Just be careful to keep your pampering fund somewhere safe unless you want your money disappearing before you ever get the chance to use it.

Is it guilt that's stopping you? Really? Do you actually believe that you should feel any guilt after everything that you have been through? Guilt, from here on out, is just not allowed. You deserve to be pampered, and so much more. You deserve respect, love, and some fun in your life. These are all things that you can give to yourself.

There are also tons of little inexpensive ways to feel pampered without ever having to worry about money. How much does a new bottle of nail polish cost? For less than five dollars, you can have all of the supplies needed for an at-home manicure and pedicure. Something as simple as a bath can leave you feeling luxurious. Turn your bath time into a spa experience. Play some soft music. Light a few candles. Make yourself a "Do Not Disturb" sign and tell your family that you are to be left alone for the next hour. As you lie in your bath, imagine that the warm water is melting away all of your cares, leaving you peaceful and radiant.

Make it a habit to turn everyday moments into special treats. When you're washing your hair, give yourself a relaxing head massage just like they do in the salons. Work up a good lather, pretend your hands belong to somebody else, and enjoy as you rub your scalp, neck, and shoulders. What an easy way to pamper yourself every day.

In the morning, as you're prepping in front of the mirror, take it as an opportunity to remind yourself how spectacular you are. Look at your reflection and admire all of your beautiful traits. This may be different from your usual self-talk. Most of us are very hard on ourselves. We easily see the beauty in other women, but for some reason, we have a difficult time acknowledging our own appeal. Rather than focusing on the brilliant color of our eyes and perfectly sculpted jawline, we zoom in on our large pores and crooked nose. When you learn to focus on your strengths, you become more confident. Compliment yourself inwardly every chance you get. Make it a daily practice.

When you're preparing dinner, you can make it a fun time. Pretend that you are a famous chef whipping up your next great creation. Light candles at the dinner table and use your fine china. Enjoy all of the beautiful things that you have. Why keep things locked away waiting for some future event to use them? All that you have is right now at this very moment.

When you can take pleasure from the simple details of daily life, then you are living richly. Being financially rich and being rich in spirit are two very different things. Money can make life easier, but it does not guarantee happiness. Even the people who seem to be living a fairytale existence from the outside are sometimes consumed with sadness. History has shown this time and time again.

When we are feeling unhappy, we typically look outside of ourselves for the cause. We blame our lack of money, our dead-end job, or our loved one's addiction for our discontentment. We believe that if our loved one would get clean once and for all then we would be happy. If we just had more money or objects, then life would be wonderful.

Most of us dream of winning the lottery and becoming an instant millionaire. We imagine how quickly all of our problems would be zapped away. Over time, though, whatever your deep inner feelings were before would return. If at your core you were an unhappy person before winning the lottery, then you would most likely be an unhappy person afterward. Your depression could even worsen as you realize that the money was never to blame.

You may believe that you would be the happiest person on earth if your loved one would get clean. There is no doubt that a lot of stress would be lifted away, but it is not the magic cure for your unhappiness. I have found that along with sobriety there are new challenges to face. Life may be easier, but it is never perfect. You can discover the joy within even in the midst of your loved one's addiction.

True happiness is acceptance. It's finding delight in the simple details. It's learning to forgive. It's having faith that your future is bright, and knowing that you will always have whatever you need.

In your journal, write down all of those things that you would love to do or accomplish over the next year. Do you want to write a book? Take an art or cooking class? Learn to play golf? Go back to school? What are those things that you always thought you would like to do when the timing was right? Well, the time to start is now.

How about today? What can you do today that would be fun? Bake cookies? Go for a bike ride? Pull out the art supplies with your kids and have fun playing like you're ten years old again?

Most of us fill our days with obligations. Even on our days off, we put ourselves to work. Walk into Home Depot on a Sunday afternoon and you see the evidence of this. The weekend becomes our chance to lay sod in the backyard, patch the cracked drywall in the hallway, scrub the shower, clean out the refrigerator, and organize our closets.

When we were kids, most of us looked forward to the weekends because it was our chance to have fun. There were no agendas or lists to complete. We did whatever we felt like, even if that meant doing nothing. Back then we had the right idea.

As adults we tend to lose our sense of spontaneity. You can get it back. Fun is not reserved for kids only. How about a picnic in the park? Spend the afternoon playing Frisbee and feeding the ducks. Remember how much fun it used to be to play dress up? It can still be fun. Spend some time going through your closet and trying on clothes. You may discover a new combination of outfits to wear, or find a top that you thought you had lost years ago. Try styling your hair in a new way. Pull out your makeup and play around with different techniques. Who cares if you end up looking liking a clown? It washes off! When was the last time you blasted your favorite music and danced around the house? Just a few minutes of upbeat music can transform you.

Have you distanced yourself from friends lately? Don't stay in isolation. Pick up the phone. Get out into the world and start living again. We are social beings born with a need for companionship. If you are looking to the addict to fulfill your need for social contact, you will become malnourished. Until he can love himself enough to get well, he will never be able to supplement your needs. You must learn to give yourself the love and attention that you desire.

I believe that you can change your life simply by changing your attitude. I have witnessed this in my own life. Sometimes though, even with a positive outlook, there may be those days that take their toll. No matter how hard you try, you can't kick the blues. On days like those, it's okay to give in. Let those emotions run their course.

Allow yourself to have a pity party. Stay in your robe, eat ice cream, cry, feel sorry for yourself, and watch old movies all day. Get it out so that you can move on. But if your sadness doesn't go away within a few days, or it begins to turn into something deeper, please seek professional help. Depression is a serious medical condition, and you shouldn't try to deal with it alone.

Taking care of yourself is about listening to your body. It is about following your instincts, and making your mental and physical health your highest priorities. Start making time in your life for *you*.

How about waking up before the rest of the household is up and enjoying your own quiet time? Make it your private ritual to watch the sun come up with a hot cup of tea. Use your alone time to write in your journal, read, or just sit in silence.

Maybe you're not a morning person. In that case, you should find a space in your home that belongs to only you—a place where you can go at any time to feel relaxed and peaceful. If you have a spare bedroom that has become a storage area, claim it as your own. Decorate it in a way that leaves you feeling inspired. Frame your favorite poems and affirmations. Paint the walls a calming color. Make sure that there is a spot for napping, reading, writing, or anything else you may want to do during your private time.

You may be thinking that your home is far too cramped and there isn't one place that you can make your own. Get creative. How about a closet? A couple of pillows and you have a cozy spot to read, write, or meditate. If you have a walk-in closet, it is probably big enough for a comfy chair and reading lamp. Move all of the clothes to one side and keep the other side for yourself.

Of course, your family may worry. "Mom has locked herself in the closet again," they'll say to each other. "She must have lost her mind." When you come back out they'll probably treat you extra nicely out of their fear of sending you over the edge. But it's okay because you know that you're not crazy. In fact, for the first time in a while you may be doing something really sane—you are spending quality time with yourself.

Putting yourself at the top of the list may feel uncomfortable at first. Maybe you can't even remember the last time that you did something just for you. The important thing is to start taking steps toward this new attitude. Taking care of yourself is not just about pampering yourself physically—it is about treating yourself with the respect that you deserve.

Pay attention to your inner dialogue. Do you speak to

yourself lovingly, or do you tend to be self-critical? Are you forgiving, or do you beat yourself up when you make a mistake? By keeping your thoughts towards yourself supportive, and making a point to treat yourself well, your self-esteem will grow strong. As your confidence grows, you will find it easier to take the steps toward change. Your fear will no longer paralyze you.

People learn to adapt to their current circumstances. Even if a situation is painful, it becomes comfortable in some ways. You at least know what to expect. The idea of change is scary because it is venturing into the unknown.

In the movie "The Shawshank Redemption," the character Grady has been in prison his entire adult life. As an old man, he is released, only to find himself wanting to return. It is the only life that he has known. Most of us would fear prison, but he fears the outside. He tries to think up ways that he can get arrested and sent back. A life in prison (what most of us would find a nightmare) has become his comfort zone. Eventually, freedom becomes so difficult for him that he makes the decision to end his own life.

Every day is filled with choices. You can decide to stay in your comfort zone, regardless of how painful it has become, or you can make the choice of change. Although change may cause some fear, the biggest risk of all is standing still. You are here to shine; to love, to laugh and—yes, to cry. Live every day to its fullest. Don't put off your dreams and goals for a better time. There is no other time; there is only now.

Journaling Suggestion:

Write a love letter to yourself. In this letter write about all of the things you have done that have made you proud. Tell yourself how beautiful you are. How funny, resilient, and smart you are. Be supportive in this letter. Don't be afraid to get too deep. Delve in. You might want to write this letter on beautiful stationary rather than your journal. When you are done, you can seal it up and keep it somewhere safe. When you are having an especially hard day, and you're feeling all alone in the world, you can pull out your letter. It may be just what you need to lift your spirits.

When you know you are doing your very best within the circumstances of your existence, applaud yourself!
–Rusty Berkus

Gratitude

Being grateful is a way of life. When you start to focus on all of the wonderful gifts that surround you, it becomes easy to stay in a positive frame of mind. You have a choice. You can choose to focus on the negative, which will no doubt leave you feeling lousy, or you can choose to focus on the positive. Realizing all of the joys in your life will keep you feeling joyous.

When you're dealing with the craziness that goes along with addiction, it may be difficult to stay in a positive frame of mind. You may feel that any situation would be better than the one you're in right now. When you start making an inventory of the things that you are grateful for, however, you will quickly see that your life is full of miracles to cherish.

Just recently, my son Jesse, who is now twenty-one, was in an accident. He was working with my husband Dean and left to grab some lunch. About fifteen minutes had passed when Dean received a phone call from him. He was obviously shaken and stated that he had just wrecked his truck. Expecting to see a dented fender, Dean drove to the spot where Jesse was.

What he saw when he reached the site shocked him. Jesse, his face covered in blood, was on a stretcher being put into an ambulance. His truck was completely totaled. He had lost control while looking for some loose change. The truck went off the road, hitting one tree, and then ricocheting into another.

As a parent, your biggest fear is of something bad happening to your children. Once they start driving, you are reminded every time they leave the house how helpless you are when it comes to their safety. You can teach them to put on their seatbelts. You can remind them to be cautious and go the speed limit, but you really have no control over what happens once they are out on the road.

When I received the phone call from Dean, I was on my way to work. I'm lucky that I didn't get into an accident myself because I don't even remember driving after that. I just recall feeling complete panic as I rushed to the hospital.

Jesse had a guardian angel watching out for him that day. Aside from a few stitches in his head, he was unharmed. Seeing the vehicle afterward was a reminder of how lucky we were. It could have been tragic. Having my son walk away from that accident is enough to keep me feeling grateful forever.

We all tend occasionally to take the people in our lives for granted. We may go weeks or even longer without talking to our parents. We have friends that we lose contact with. Our children grow up, and move out of our homes, and we go on with our lives. The accident served as a reminder to me of just how blessed I am.

I realized that I sometimes allowed days to go by without talking to Jesse. I didn't want to be the bothersome mom calling her grown son. Now I make sure to touch base with him every day, even if it's just a two-minute call, to tell him how much I love him.

Life is a gift. A gift that most of us take for granted. If you were to find out that you only had one month left to live, you would see things very differently. You would cherish each moment that you had with the people you love. You would say the things that you want to say. You would appreciate the simple things in life, such as the color of the sky right before the sun sets, the feel of moist grass on your bare feet, a hug from your child. You would have a new appreciation for everything in life because you would realize that this might be the last time you experience it. This is how we should be living our lives every day.

Make it a new habit to spend the first few minutes of each morning giving thanks for all of the things that you are grateful for. You should do this before you even get out of bed. Open your eyes and have your first thoughts of the day start you out in a grateful state. *Thank you for this fresh new day. Thank you for my health. Thank you for this warm bed that gave me a great night's sleep. Thank you for my family and friends. Thank you for all of the beauty that awaits me today.*

When you begin your day feeling grateful, you set yourself up for a glorious day. From the moment you step out of bed, you are in grateful mode. You notice the smile that seems to appear on your dog's face, so happy to see you. Your warm shower feels especially soothing. You smell the aroma of coffee coming from the kitchen and it fills your senses. As you take your first sip, you can't remember it ever tasting so delicious. You step outside and notice how exhilarating the cool breeze of a new day feels against your skin. You catch every green light, and when you arrive to work a parking space is at the very front waiting for you. Okay, maybe you don't always get the green lights and parking spaces, but when you stay focused on the good stuff, more of it appears to come your way.

It is easy to get caught up in complaining. It has actually become a national pastime in our society. Listen to a typical phone conversation between friends and you might hear something like this:

"Hey, Bridget, how's it going?"

"Oh, it's been better. My asthma has been acting up again and the kids all have the flu."

"I'm just getting over the flu myself. I thought I was going to die last week, I was so sick. How is work going?"

"Well, you know that promotion I've been working so hard for? They gave it to some woman who just started with the company two months ago. I'm telling you, I've had it. I'm ready to quit that job."

"You should just be happy that you have a job. I'm going so stir crazy in this house. I'd do anything to get back out into the real world again."

"The real world is exhausting. I just feel tired all of the time. You're lucky that you have a husband who supports you staying home."

"It wouldn't be so bad if Gary wasn't so controlling. He acts more like my father then a husband. I'd trade husbands any day."

"Do you want to go to lunch tomorrow?"

"I would but I just have too much to do. I can't seem to find the time to even breathe lately."

"Well, I'd better go. I hear the kids fighting and I need to break it up before somebody gets hurt."

"Okay, I'll talk to you later."

Start paying attention to the conversations that you share with family and friends. You might find that this example sounds familiar. It's as if there is some kind of competition to find out whose life is more miserable. It's easy to take on the victim role. We blame the world for all of our problems. The more we focus on how terrible our life is, the worse it seems to get.

Complaining is a toxic habit. When you are complaining or whining, then you are focusing on the negative. Being in that mind state will only cause more bad stuff to come your way.

We've all experienced waking up on the wrong side of the bed. Maybe your alarm doesn't go off and it sets in motion the tone for the rest of the day. From the moment you open your eyes, you're panicked and anxious and everything you touch turns sour. You discover that you forgot to switch the laundry the night before so every towel in the house is wet. Your dog peed on the carpet because nobody was up to let him out. You go to start your car and the battery is dead. On days like this, you definitely don't catch the green lights, and the only parking spaces are in the very back row.

When you find yourself getting sucked into one of these negative spirals, you can turns things around simply by switching gears. Your attitude works like a magnet. Take a deep breath and start over before you invite any more chaos.

We are all faced with challenges but we make the choice of how we handle them. We can even learn to be grateful for those challenges. They help us to grow and evolve. It is the sum of all of our experiences that creates who we are.

Imagine living your entire life without any obstacles. Everything that you ever wanted you received. You never had to work for it. You never had to wait. You never had an argument. You never got sick or hurt. You never had anybody you love get sick or hurt. You never felt nervous or scared. Everything was always perfect.

We all desire a life filled with peace, comfort, and security, but if we only experienced those things we would be cheated of so much. How would you ever feel success if you didn't have some struggles to overcome? How would you know true joy if you never felt sadness? Would you want to go your entire life without ever feeling exhausted from a hard day's work? Never having the feeling of butterflies in your stomach? Never experiencing the release of anger? Never feeling the fear of vulnerability?

You can learn to appreciate every part of your life, even the challenges. I once had a neighbor who appeared to have so many struggles. Her grown son was disabled and unable to care for himself. She had custody of her young grandchild because her daughter was in jail. Her husband had a disability of his own, and financially, they barely made it each month.

One day I commented to her that it seemed unfair how many obstacles she had in her life. "Don't feel sorry for me," she replied. "I am a strong woman and God knows this. That is why he has given me so many responsibilities. I feel like the lucky one. I love my life because it has so much meaning."

I was impressed by how she reflected on her challenges in

such a positive way. She could have easily taken on the victim role and felt sorry for herself. What most of us would see as downfalls, she saw as opportunities from God.

There are people who defy odds every day. They are strong when others would give up. Take, for example, the disease of cancer. Some people get cancer and see it as a calling to make positive changes. As a result, their relationships grow stronger, they become more spiritual, and they find new meaning in their lives. Their cancer is no different from anyone else's, but they choose to see the lessons that have come with it. They are a source of inspiration to those around them.

Dealing with addiction is tough, but don't lose perspective. There are situations that would be worse. People deal with tragedy every day. There are some who place blame on others and feel sorry for themselves. Then there are those who face their circumstances with grace. You make the choice of how you face yours.

As you continue to focus on being grateful, life gets easier. The struggles may be the same but you see them in a different light. At the same time, be easy on yourself when you allow old feelings to return. Fear, jealousy, and self-absorption are normal human reactions, and they can sneak their way in regardless of how hard you try to avoid them. As you improve your frame of mind, you will be able to catch them faster and remove them before they infect you.

When you start feeling like a victim, you can stop and give yourself an attitude adjustment. When you find the green monster of envy inviting itself in, you can realize what's happening and show it to the door. You can choose to change your viewpoint when you feel like the world is falling down around you. You can cut ties with your fears and let them go.

Most of us are not asking for, nor expecting, perfection in our lives. We accept that difficulties occur. But for those of us who love an addict, we would just like to have the "normal" problems that other couples seem to have. Dirty towels left on the bathroom floor, not agreeing on whose turn it is to do the dishes, the power struggle over the remote control—we could deal with those problems all day long.

Hopefully, the day will come when your loved one gets the help that he needs. Eventually you may feel like that "normal" couple. But even if that day does not come, your new attitude towards life will give you the courage to walk away from an unhealthy lifestyle, and you will be grateful for your new strength.

Celebrate your life—that you are here, that you are a survivor, that you have people in your life who love you. Celebrate the brilliant stars that light up the sky, the single dandelion that grew through the crack on your porch, having air conditioning in the middle of summer, laughter, friendships, family. Celebrate because you have so much to be grateful for.

Journaling Suggestion:

I encourage you to start a gratitude journal. In this journal, start listing all of the things that you are grateful for. It is easy to do once you start; your children, your eyesight, a roof over your head, running water. Keep going until you can't think of anything else. Keep your journal close by and whenever something else pops into your head, add it to your list. As you do this you will notice that you are staying focused on all of the "positives" in your life. You can start to see what a difference this can make in your attitude. Your gratitude journal should be an ongoing project. Make it your goal to fill every page. The more you think about things in your life to be grateful for, the easier it becomes. A great way to start your day is to add a few items to your list. When your day is coming to an end, you can once again add some items before going to bed. Whenever you are feeling down, you can pull out your gratitude journal. As you read through its pages, you will be reminded of just how lucky you are.

We tend to forget that happiness doesn't come as
a result of getting something we don't have, but rather
of recognizing and appreciating what we do have.
-Frederick Keonig

The Power of Prayer

When I first began my recovery from co-addiction, getting strong was my main goal. But at times I found that along with my new strength came sadness. While I was feeling excitement from the spark lit inside myself, I also felt deep sorrow for my husband who was stuck in his world of addiction.

There was one night that I was overcome with the feeling of grief. It broke my heart to see my husband in such bad shape. He barely resembled the man that I had fallen in love with. His body looked weak and sickly. His eyes were dark and without life. I couldn't even remember the last time that he cracked a smile.

There was such a distance growing between us that part of me wanted to go back to the way things were. I felt guilty, as though I were saving myself from a sinking ship but leaving him behind to drown. I watched him falling deeper and deeper into depression. I wanted so badly to give him some of my strength, but there seemed to be no reaching him at this point. In many ways, it was as though my husband had died.

I felt completely helpless. I lay in bed and cried until there wasn't a tear left in me. When the crying stopped, I started to pray. There was nothing else left for me to do.

I prayed for guidance to help me make the right decisions.

I prayed for my husband to gain strength over his addiction so that I could have the man I loved back. I continued to pray for some time when I started to see visions of angels coming into my mind. There were so many of them that I stopped praying and started focusing on them. One by one, they each came forward gently smiling as if to tell me that everything was going to be alright. Then a much larger angel came into view. The other angels all parted off to the side as she floated in and hovered right above me. She was so clear in my mind and I could see every detail of her face. I looked into her caring eyes and felt a sense of calm. I once again started to pray.

As I was in the middle of praying, Dean came to bed. This was a surprise to me because most nights he would eventually pass out on the couch. He rarely came to sleep in our bed anymore. As he climbed in, I pictured the angel floating directly above him. I could see her lovingly watching him. As I rolled over to go to sleep, I felt a reassuring peacefulness.

No more than a couple of minutes passed when Dean suddenly threw the covers off and jumped out of bed.

"Oh, my God, oh, my God!" he kept repeating as he got up and walked out of the room.

"What is it?" I responded, getting up to follow him.

He sat down on the couch and slumped over, putting his head into his hands. He rubbed his head as if trying to make sense of what just happened.

"Dean, what is it?" I asked, completely confused by what was going on.

He looked up at me, his eyes in disbelief, and stated, "I'm cured."

"What?" I asked.

"I'm cured." he said. "It's gone. I don't know what just happened, but I can feel it. It's like everything has just been lifted off me."

As he was sharing this, I started thinking about the angel. Was it possible that Dean felt her presence? Was she more than my imagination? It seemed unbelievable, but I could think of no other explanation.

I knelt down in front of him and looked into his eyes. "Dean, you're not going to believe this, but let me tell you what I was doing right before you came to bed".

I then proceeded to tell him how I was praying and saw the vision of angels. I told him about the angel that was watching over him. We were both overwhelmed by what had just happened. He kept telling me how wonderful he felt. How he hadn't felt like that in years and he just knew that he would never use again. He had such a feeling of bliss that we sat up for a couple of hours just talking about it. The power of prayer was undeniable to both of us at that moment. That night I had my husband back, just as I had prayed for.

I would like to say that all of Dean's addiction problems ended there. Unfortunately, that feeling eventually wore off and he did use again, but I do believe it was a beginning point to his recovery. The lesson that we both learned that night was powerful. We knew that a special energy was there with us. It touched Dean deeply and took all of his pain away, at least temporarily. Incredibly, it was there simply because I had asked.

It was when my son was born that prayer became a regular practice in my life. Your love for your children is different from any other love. It is truly unconditional. From the moment they take their first breaths, you want nothing but the best for them. Suddenly the world seems far scarier than it ever did before. You are now responsible for their well-being and it can be terrifying. There are so many things that you have no control over, so you are only left with faith to keep you from feeling helpless.

When it came to my husband's addiction, however, I rarely turned to prayer for help. Maybe it was because I was filled with rage so much of the time that praying for him seemed like the last thing I wanted to do. I admit that there were times when I wished he would die because living with his addiction was so unbearable and I could see no other way out.

When two people are sharing their lives together, they have the ability to hurt each other far more deeply than anyone else ever could. Nothing can erase what has been done. Forgiveness is the only way to move on. Prayer has a magical way of softening the hardness in your heart and making it easier to forgive. The loving feelings that you once felt for that person find their way back in.

After the experience with the angels, I started praying for my husband regularly. I found that during times of anger, if I stopped and prayed for my husband, my negative feelings lifted. I instantly felt better inside. By praying, I saw my husband through loving eyes. The prayers always seemed to help the situation. Maybe my prayers were being answered, or maybe it was a matter of seeing things in a different light, or perhaps it was a combination of both. It doesn't really matter how or why it works, only that it does.

Most of us pray. We may have different religions, but the act of prayer is almost universal. A Newsweek cover story revealed that ninety-one percent of all women and eighty-five percent of all men pray. It seems to be a natural human instinct. You could travel to the far reaches of the earth and find a remote village where the people have never been exposed to any outside influences, yet undoubtedly you will find that some form of prayer is part of their culture.

Prayer is personal and we each do it in our own unique way. Some of us learned certain prayers that we repeated when we were younger and we still repeat those same prayers today. Some of us meditate and that is our form of prayer. Some of us have entire conversations with God.

When my son Jesse was about eight years old, I gave him his own journal. He had always watched me write in mine, and now that he was learning to write, I felt it would be a good practice for him to get into. When I gave it to him, I explained that there was no right or wrong way to use his journal. He could write about his day, or write about his feelings, or even write poems or stories if that's what he felt like.

About a week went by when I asked him if he was enjoying his journal.

"Yes," he told me. "Do you want to see what I've written?"

"Only if you want to share it," I said.

He pulled his journal out of the top drawer of his dresser and brought it over to me. The first couple of entries were short and simple. They quickly summarized what he did for the day, and I could tell that he was having a hard time getting his thoughts down on paper. But the next three entries filled my heart. They were prayers written in letter form to God.

I felt so proud of him at that moment. It was never my suggestion for him to write down his prayers; it was just something he naturally did on his own. I thought it was such a great idea that I even started writing prayers in my own journal.

Prayers are answered every day, and when you open your mind up to seeing it, you can find the evidence all around you. There was one Sunday morning when I woke up with the urge to clean out closets. This was not the kind of thing I typically liked to do, but the impulse hit so I went with it. As I cleaned out my son's closet, I came across quite a few pairs of jeans and many shirts that he had recently outgrown. I set them all aside in a stack to take to the Goodwill Center.

Later that day, my son's friend came over. He was built smaller than my son so I asked him to try on some of the clothes. They were a perfect fit and when he left, I sent the stack of clothes with him. A short time later I received a phone call from his mother. I could hear in her voice that she was emotional. She told me how thankful she was for the clothing. She went on to tell me how she had just prayed the night before for some way to buy clothes for her son. He had outgrown most of his existing clothes and money was too tight to afford new ones. When her son walked in the house, his arms filled with clothing, she was amazed. She told me that I was her angel on earth.

I realized that on that particular day, I *was* a part of the design to answer her prayers. It got me thinking. How many times are we are a part of a bigger plan? How many times are we in fact angels on earth and we don't even realize it?

There have been many times when I felt that I was a part of my husband's life for a reason. That I was brought into his life to somehow help him. And that may very well be the case. At the same time, he may have been brought into my life to help me. My relationship with him has taught me many lessons and I have grown spiritually because of them.

We all have the ability to help each other in this life, but unfortunately, we can't rescue our loved ones from addiction. We are only human after all and we do not have that kind of power. When it comes to being with a person who is ill with disease or addiction, prayer is sometimes the only way that we can help them. In Al-Anon they have the saying, "Let go and let God." It is a reminder that we do not always have control over a situation. That we have to learn to give that control over to a higher power and have faith that there is a reason, a purpose, and a plan in place. Each Al-Anon meeting ends with the Serenity Prayer:

> *God, grant me the serenity*
> *To accept the things I cannot change;*
> *The courage to change the things I can;*
> *And the wisdom to know the difference.*

Having faith can free you. Understanding that you are not supposed to be the one with all of the answers can be a huge weight off your shoulders. You are here to live *your* life. You are not responsible for the choices that your loved one makes and it is unhealthy for you to take those choices personally. It is not the person that you love making poor decisions, it is the addiction.

I'm not trying to make excuses for the addict. I know how angry you feel much of the time. I encourage you to at least try letting go of your anger and spend some time praying for him.

Do what you can to detach yourself from his problems and start having faith that there is a plan for him.

In the process, don't forget to pray for yourself. You need answers. You need help. Ask for guidance, and then be open to receiving the suggestions. Look for the clues that come your way. Maybe you wake up and vividly remember a dream that gives you some insight. Out of the blue you receive an unexpected job offer that excites you. A friend from out of town calls and suggests that you take a trip out to see her. Stop seeing these situations as random and start looking at them more closely. Maybe you're receiving the guidance that you asked for.

Journaling Suggestion:

Write a letter to God or your Higher Power. In this letter, share your fears and ask for guidance. You may find that when you write a letter like this before going to sleep, you sometimes receive the answers you're looking for in your dreams, or you may wake up with a new insight. You don't always have to ask for something in your letters; one of the highest forms of prayer is sharing your gratitude for all of the gifts in your life. When there is friction between you and your loved one, instead of reacting, try stepping aside and writing a prayer. At first it might be difficult to let your anger go long enough to do this, but you will probably find that the anger will naturally subside once you start. When you're done, attempt to quiet your mind long enough to listen for guidance coming from within. Then write about the effect that this had on the situation.

You need not cry very loud;
He is nearer to us than we think.
-Brother Lawrence

Harnessing Your Inner Strength

There is no power greater than the power of inner strength. When you are dealing with the problems of addiction, however, they can chip away at your confidence and leave you feeling weak inside. The good news is that you can build it back up like a muscle—the workouts are just a bit different.

What is inner strength? It is the power inside that pushes you into action even when you're scared, that allows other peoples' behaviors and comments to roll off your back no matter how hurtful they may be, that gives you the willpower to accomplish your goals regardless of how large they are. Inner strength comes from having a close connection to your spirit.

The more in tune you are to the voice inside of you, the stronger you will be. People call that inner voice many different things: intuition, Higher Power, God, or you may call it something else altogether. It doesn't matter what you name it, as long as you build a close relationship to it.

One of the best ways to grow that relationship is through meditation. If you have never meditated before you may have a misconception about it. Many people are turned off by meditation because they see it as New Age or religious. While it does play an important role in many religions, it is not necessarily a religious act (unless you choose to make it one).

Meditation is simply the practice of quieting the mind.

Our minds are constantly going. Most of the time we are unaware of just how much clatter goes on. Your mind is like a hyperactive child who's constantly bored and looking for something to keep it busy. While you're going along with your day, it's off doing its own thing. You may be driving to work but it's having fun singing "The Brady Bunch" theme song. You're cooking dinner but it's obsessing about the sarcastic comment your husband made yesterday. You're in the middle of taking a shower but it's busy imagining giant spiders and snakes crawling up from the drain. All the while you have become so used to the chaos that you are almost oblivious to it.

When you meditate, you become aware of this internal free-for-all. At first it can be difficult to calm it down, but just like anything, it gets easier with practice. As you get better at quieting your mind, you become more aware of those times when it's getting out of control. Instead of ignoring it, you start teaching it some boundaries. They say that spoiled children actually desire some discipline. Well, your mind is like that spoiled child, and it will thrive in its new peaceful environment.

Once you learn to quiet your mind, it becomes easier to listen to your inner voice. That voice is different from the chattering voice of your mind. Your inner voice comes from deep inside. It may come to you more as a feeling than words. Over time, as you get to know it better, you will learn its language.

There are many types of meditation, and while I am not an expert on all of these, I have learned enough to understand its benefits: increased circulation of oxygen, strengthened immunity, improved focus and concentration, and a greater sense of awareness, to name just a few.

The benefits that I've received through meditation have been so great that I felt it was important to share my experience. With all of the positive changes I made towards my recovery from co-addiction, meditation was one of the greatest. Through meditation I found a connection to my spirit that I never had before.

The way I meditate may be different from the way some teachers of meditation would instruct. I have combined what I've learned with what makes me feel comfortable. I personally believe that there are no rules. You should follow your instincts and do what feels natural to you. You may come up with your own unique way of meditating, and if you do, you should go for it.

I find that one of the best times for me to meditate is in bed, right before going to sleep. This way nobody needs to know what's going on and it allows for a comfortable position (lying down). Start out by taking several deep breaths. As you inhale, imagine that you are breathing in pure energy. You might picture the energy as beautiful stardust. As you exhale, imagine that you are releasing all of your tension and worries. You can see these as pictures of your problems or you might just imagine a light smoke leaving your body and floating away.

Next visualize a bright light entering through the top of your head. As you breathe in and out, feel the light slowly working its way through your body. It moves its way through your head and neck, down your arms, into your breasts and back, through your torso and buttocks, and finally down each of your legs. Feel the warm light relaxing all of your muscles, leaving you peaceful.

Now that you are in a calm state, simply stay still and focus on your breathing. Take in full, deep breaths. As thoughts enter your mind acknowledge them and quickly send them away. Eventually the thoughts will get tired of being pushed away and stop coming. That is when you know that you've reached your ultimate desired state—when you are lying in pure silence and your mind is completely clear. At first the silence may only last for seconds at a time, but as you practice more, the silence will grow longer.

Sometimes, in the middle of the silence, an important thought or idea will enter your mind. This is different from the meaningless chatter. Maybe you've been worried about a particular problem and suddenly you see a clear answer. This is your inner guide speaking to you. You may decide to use the rest of your meditation time to think about this new idea. Some might see this as defeating the purpose of meditation (clearing the mind), but if you send the thought away too quickly you might risk losing this new insight. Remember, there is no "right" or "wrong" in meditation.

You may lose all awareness and fall asleep. I see this as a good thing. Instead of falling asleep with your daily thoughts and problems swimming around in your head, you fall asleep in a purely peaceful state. On nights like these, you may find that you sleep more soundly and your dreams are more vivid and detailed.

Walking is another time that can be good for meditating. As you are walking, attempt to keep your mind clear. Once again, as thoughts enter your mind, acknowledge them and send them away. Stay focused on your breathing and listen to the natural sounds around you. You might want to keep a small piece of paper and pen in your pocket; that way you can write down any messages that you believe are coming from your inner guide. Once you get them down on paper you can let them go and continue on your meditation walk.

When you meditate regularly, you find an inner peace that eventually stays with you long past your meditation period. That's really the idea—to reach a state of serenity during all of your waking hours. After all, it's easy to feel peaceful during fifteen minutes of meditation, but if an hour later you find yourself honking and screaming at the driver in front of you in a fit of road rage, then those few minutes in meditation have done little to make a difference. That is why it is so important to keep it a regular practice—so that you can eventually be in tune with your spirit twenty-four hours a day.

As you get closer to your spiritual side you will learn to trust your instincts—those gut feelings you get about people and circumstances. When you are in tune, your instincts are rarely (if ever) wrong. Unfortunately, families of addicts tend to deny their gut feelings and instead choose to fall for the same lies over and over again.

You don't want to believe that your loved one would choose to lie to you. He couldn't possibly be lying if he just swore on your life, could he? He promises up and down that he owes sixty dollars to his dealer. Once he pays this debt, he will be free and clear and he will never touch another drug again. He's ready to quit, he tells you. Your instincts warn you that he's lying, but you choose not to listen. Instead you believe the certainty in his voice. You want so badly to trust him.

So off to the ATM machine you go to get the money that will pay off the dealer and leave you both free to start your new life together. Never mind that he said the same thing the night before and instead came home high. Not to mention the ten other times he told you the same lie in the last month, and each of those times came home high. This time is different, right?

Addicts lie. You can walk in on an addict shooting up, the needle deep in his skin, and he will insist with conviction that he isn't doing drugs. As long as he is addicted, he will never be trustworthy. Your instincts have always known this. As you build your inner strength, you will listen more closely to these instincts and you will no longer set yourself up for disappointment. You might still choose to hand him the money he's requesting, but you will know that he is lying regardless of what he says.

Your instincts speak to you through your feelings. When you get tired of being hurt over and over, you may squash those feelings down because they've become too painful, but as you do this you disconnect. Your feelings are full of wisdom and they speak the truth. Many times, the pain you end up dealing with comes from ignoring its warnings. Your instincts tell you not to believe the lies, or they caution you to avoid certain situations, but because you don't like what they have to say, you ignore them. You ignore the flip-flopping in your stomach, the aching feeling in your heart, the voice screaming deep inside.

Eventually, if you continue ignoring your feelings, they will find other ways to get your attention. They will show up as stomach disorders, heart problems, weight issues, or other diseases. You will be healthier and happier if you listen more closely the first time around. It's an easy language to understand: when you are feeling good, your inner guide is telling you that you're on the right path; when you are feeling bad, it's a warning sign to change course. Trust in your feelings. Your inner guide will never lead you astray.

Another way that your inner guide will speak to you is through your dreams. Some people don't think that they dream, but everybody does. Many times dreams are just forgotten within moments of waking up. It is a good idea to keep a notepad and pen close to your bedside for those times when you wake up and recall a dream. Don't worry about figuring out its meaning right then, just write down any details that you can remember. You can go back later, when you are wide awake, and look for any messages.

There is no doubt that many dreams seem to be nothing but silliness. Maybe you dream that you're having a picnic with Daffy Duck and Papa Smurf. You all finish eating and then climb into a hot air balloon that turns into a rocket ship and flies away. What could that possibly mean? Maybe it means nothing, but it sure makes sleeping fun!

Then there are the dreams that stick with you. The ones you think about all day long—and sometimes even days or weeks after. These dreams are carrying a message. I had a dream like this when my husband was deep into his addiction. Even now, years later, I get a sinking feeling just thinking about it.

In this dream, I woke in the middle of the night to find that Dean wasn't in bed. I could hear a loud buzzing sound coming from outside, so I got up to investigate. As I looked out into the back yard, I could see a spotlight hanging down from a large oak tree. Under the light my husband was working on something. He had a table saw set up under the tree and was consumed in his project. I couldn't imagine what he would be working on at that time of night, so I walked outside to find out.

As I got closer he didn't notice my presence. I called out his name but the saw was too noisy and overpowered my voice. I yelled his name more loudly and that time he looked up with a crazed fear in his eyes.

I glanced over to see the bloody torso of a woman lying on the table saw. Several of her limbs were scattered on the ground. Shocked and in disbelief, my world began to spin. I tried to register in my mind what I had just discovered. Did my husband kill this woman? How could this be happening?

I heard a rustling sound coming from behind my husband and noticed that our neighbor was looking over the fence. I looked into the man's eyes and instantly knew that he would be calling the police. I started to panic and told my husband that we needed to hide the body. So suddenly, there I was, helping him dig a hole to bury this woman's remains.

As we dug up the dirt, other limbs and body parts started to come to the surface. Some were obviously old because they were pure bone, but others looked fresh. You could still see the blood and skin. Our yard was filled with the remains of women. How many times had he killed? My biggest fear at that point was getting caught. If we didn't get this all covered up before the police arrived, the entire world would know what he'd been doing.

We finished burying the last of the evidence just before the sound of sirens filled the air. When I answered the door I acted as though everything were perfectly fine, but the police knew better and gave me a truth serum to get me to talk. As soon as I took the serum the truth came out. I immediately felt a sense of relief. As I watched them take my husband away I realized just how disturbed he was.

When I woke up I was sick to my stomach. I couldn't even talk to my husband because I was so upset. I knew it was a dream, but it all felt so real. The sick feeling stuck with me for days.

As I attempted to analyze my dream it became clear to me what the message was. At first I couldn't figure out all of the dead women. But then I realized that the women in the dream were all me. They represented the many times my husband's addiction tore my heart out and left me feeling dead inside. In the dream I did exactly what I did in real life—I helped him to cover up the evidence. The dream showed me that I had become so fearful of our family and friends knowing the truth that I was willing to help him hide his addiction.

The thing that really stuck with me was the sense of relief I felt when the truth came out. More than anything I believe this was the message intended. This dream came to me as I was starting to make progress on my new path of recovery from co-addiction. It was shortly after this dream that I gathered the courage to do exactly what it was suggesting. I opened up to my family and let the secret out.

I was able to make sense of this dream because I looked at it with an open mind. If I had taken my dream literally, I would have believed that my husband was a serial killer. I would have found myself digging up my garden, looking for the evidence that my dream had warned me about. The messages contained in your dreams are often revealed through symbols and codes, which can make them challenging to understand. The trick is learning to make sense of this symbolic language.

Some codes will be personal to each dreamer. Others are more universal. For example, dreams of falling are very common. Many times the dreamer has reached some heights in their personal or professional life and may now be afraid of failure. Another dream that most people have experienced is being naked in public. This could represent your fear of being exposed. As you begin paying attention to your dreams, you will notice this symbolic language showing up. The meanings are often not clear-cut. They will depend on each person and what is going on in his or her life.

There are many books and online resources that can help you learn about the language of dreams, but don't underestimate your own ability to break the codes. You know better than anybody what your current fears, concerns, or circumstances are.

Many of the books available are designed like dictionaries. You look up the symbol and it tells you its meaning. I once dreamt that I was in the middle of a large thunderstorm. I looked up the meaning of thunder in one of these books. It stated that thunder meant you were passing gas. I found this quite funny. How could the author of this book possibly know that?

I could imagine a laboratory where some guy is hooked up to a bunch of wires and machines while he sleeps. He is surrounded by a room full of scientists making notes about his vital signs and movements. Suddenly he lets out a fart and all of the scientists rush to wake him up.

"Quick," one of the scientists exclaims, "What were you just dreaming about?"

Still half asleep, the startled man tries to recall his dream. "Gosh, the only thing I remember is thunder," he answers back.

"Ah hah!" the excited scientist proclaims. "So that is what thunder means."

Don't lose sight of your own ability to interpret your dreams. These books can be helpful in understanding dream symbols, but there are no clear-cut answers that you will find in a book. Your dreams enable you to delve deep into your subconscious mind. While they may be difficult to decipher, don't make the mistake of dismissing their importance. Take special notice of any dreams that are recurring or those that leave a lasting impression. Dreaming gives your inner guide an opportunity to communicate with you. By paying attention to its messages, you are offered a greater understanding of yourself.

You were born with an inner wisdom. You have the tools that you need for survival right inside of yourself. Look at any animal in nature and you will understand this power. If you've ever watched a dog giving birth to its litter, you've observed that it knows exactly what to do. It lovingly cleans off each newborn pup. It lies patiently allowing them to nurse. It did not go to birthing classes. It knows to follow its instincts.

Ants create colonies. Spiders spin webs. Birds build nests. Wolves run in packs. They all have an inner guide telling them exactly what to do. They don't question or doubt it. They are in tune with their instincts; therefore, they continue to survive.

As human beings we are by far the most advanced of any creatures that exist on earth. Sadly, through our incredible achievements in science, medicine, and technology, we have lost sight of the most powerful knowledge that exists. We are so consumed with the distractions of television, computers, and telephones that we can barely hear our inner voice anymore. Many of us don't even realize it exists. When we hear its calls, we get confused.

We get an aching feeling in the pit of our stomach and think we must be hungry, so we eat. Our body feels tired but we are too busy to sleep so we consume caffeine. We sense a void deep inside of ourselves, so we shop to fill it back up. We have a frightening dream, and we're relieved when we wake up so that we can quickly block it out and go on with our day.

We often confuse sex with love, food with comfort, and money with happiness. Advertisements and celebrities teach us what success is and we believe them, instead of following our own hearts. It is time for us to take back our own power.

You are a shining spirit. Your outer world may be dark at times. It may attempt to cover your light and dim it, but your spirit is strong and bright. When you let go of your fears and doubts, and turn your trust over to your inner wisdom, your light becomes focused and clearly illuminates your way.

Quiet your mind and listen to your voice within. It will tell you everything you need to know. Pay close attention to your feelings; they will guide you to the right decisions. Be aware of your dreams; they are your subconscious speaking to you. Harness your power of inner strength and there will be nothing that can ever hold you down.

Journaling Suggestion:

Start recording your dreams. Keep your journal or a notepad and pen close to your bedside. As soon as you awake, write down any dream memories that you have. Don't delay your writing. Even vivid dreams tend to fade or become distorted quickly after waking. Record any details you can recall. Try to remember any emotions that you had during your dreaming and make sure to write those down as well. It is a good idea to date each entry in your journal. As you accumulate more and more entries, your journal will become a great source of insight. Look for any connections between your dreams and the real events of your life and notice any recurring themes. With time, you will learn the language of your dreams, making it easier to interpret their meanings. You may also find that as you give more attention to your dreams, they will respond by becoming more insightful and memorable.

*Go within every day and find the inner strength
so that the world will not blow your candle out.*
-Katherine Dunham

Guided Meditation

The following meditation is designed to get you in touch with your inner guide. There are several ways that you can do this guided meditation:

- You can read through it first then complete the meditation, making changes where you see fit.

- You can record the meditation and use the recording to lead you through the exercise. Be sure to leave a sufficient pause in your recording wherever appropriate. You can also download a free audio of this meditation at www.soaringabovecoaddiction.com

- You can have a close friend read the meditation out loud as you follow the steps.

You will want to try this meditation exercise during a time when you will not be interrupted. Your relaxation can be enhanced by playing soft music. Be sure to avoid any tight or confining clothing during your meditation time. Find a comfortable position where your back is well-supported and the room is a pleasant temperature. If you have a reclining chair, this can work perfectly.

After you've gotten into a comfortable position, close your eyes. Take a deep breath and hold it in for a few seconds. When you exhale, be sure to release all of the air from your lungs before you breathe in again. Continue breathing in this exaggerated way for five to ten breaths.

Now focus on your feet. Imagine a warm glowing light relaxing the muscles of your feet and toes...it now moves its way up to your ankles...once your ankles are relaxed, it moves its way to your calves...and now up to your knees...it slowly moves into your thighs...feel the warm light soothing any tension.

After both of your legs are feeling completely relaxed, allow the light to work its way to your buttocks...your abdomen... through your back...and your chest...allowing as much time as needed to completely relax each muscle.

Next focus on your arms...the light makes its way down both of your arms and into your hands...now let the light drift into your shoulders...to your neck...it now moves into your jaw...and face. Allow plenty of time at each of your eye sockets to release any tension still lingering...it finally moves its way through the top of your head and out each of your ear canals.

Take a moment to mentally scan your body searching for any areas that may still feel tense. Send the warm light back to any of these areas until the tension has been released. Notice how calm and peaceful your body feels.

Now imagine that you are walking down a path and in the distance you see a beautiful bridge. You start to walk towards it and as you get closer, you catch a glimpse of the other side. It is too hidden to clearly see, but it appears that the bridge leads to a garden. You feel excited at the idea of walking to the other side to explore. You come to the foot of the bridge and there is a gate at the entrance. A sign is posted on the front of the gate that reads, *Problems and Worries are not allowed to cross this bridge.*

You see a basket that is sitting off to the side of the gate with a lid labeled, *Problems and Worries.* Imagine that you place all of your problems and worries into the basket and close the lid. Notice how light and free you now feel. Suddenly the gate magically opens. As you make your way across you can already smell the fresh aroma of flowers and you hear the soft sound of a babbling brook running below.

When you reach the other side, your eyes take in a feast of beauty. Everywhere you look there are huge shade trees, clear streams and lakes, and colorful flowers. The ground is covered in lush green grass. You take off your shoes so that you can enjoy the feel of cool, soft grass between your toes.

Notice how perfectly comfortable the air feels as a soft breeze blows your way. Know that you have this place all to yourself so you are free to do whatever you like. You can swim naked in the warm lake, relax in a hammock nestled among the trees, or go exploring. If you get hungry you can snack on the ripe fruits growing all around you.

This is your private sanctuary. It belongs to you. You are free to create whatever you wish here. Maybe beyond the trees is a white sandy beach that frames clear blue water as far as the eyes can see. How about a beautiful waterfall cascading down a mountainside? Perhaps you want a giant tree house of your own design. You can have all of these things and more. Just know that when you are here you are safe. Take some time now to explore your new surroundings...

When you are ready, find a comfortable spot to sit down. As you sit there, you notice a hot air balloon descending from the sky above. It is the most beautiful hot air balloon that you have ever seen. It slowly lands in the middle of your garden. A radiant being steps out and makes its way towards you. You can feel its loving energy all around. As it gets closer, you may be able to see what it looks like or you may just sense its presence. Know that it is here for you—to help and advise you. This is a wise and all-knowing guide.

Your guide takes hold of your hand and leads you to the hot air balloon. You both step into the basket as it lifts up into the sky. You float far above your sanctuary. You drift for many miles, taking in all of the scenery. As you look down at the world below, you are overcome with its beauty.

Eventually you find yourself floating directly above your home. Your guide points down and there you see your loved one (the addict in your life). You find that looking down at your partner from this viewpoint allows you to see him in a different light. You are filled with love for him. All of your anger is gone. All of your sadness is gone. You now see him with a new understanding. Spend some time watching him through loving eyes...

Take this opportunity to ask if there are any messages or advice that your guide has for you. Open yourself up to hearing or sensing the response. Do you have any questions you would like answered? Go ahead and ask those questions now. Take some time to listen to your guide's wisdom...

You now begin to travel back toward your sanctuary. You see the bridge off in the distance as you make your descent down and safely land. As you step out, your guide is now telling you goodbye. Know that anytime you wish, your guide will return for you. Wave goodbye and watch as the hot air balloon floats away into the distance.

Before heading back, take another look around at all of the beauty that surrounds you here. Remember that this is your private sanctuary and you can return whenever you choose. Make your way back across the bridge now feeling completely calm and peaceful. Take with you any messages or insights your guide shared with you during your visit. When you reach the other side of the bridge, you decide to leave your problems and worries in the basket where you left them. Feel pride in knowing that you are confident enough to leave them behind.

Start to focus on your body now, noticing how it feels. Allow each of your muscles to slowly wake up and when you are ready, open your eyes.

Journaling Suggestion:

Write about the guide that you met during your meditation. Were you able to see a clear picture of what your guide looks like? Were you given any messages? Did you receive answers to any questions? Now that you have tried this exercise, you can continue visiting your sanctuary whenever you choose. Any time that you want answers from your inner guide all you need to do is ask.

Within your heart, keep one still,
secret spot where dreams may go.
-Louise Driscoll

Reaching Out for Help

Why is it that the families of addicts seem to have such a difficult time reaching out for help? For me it had a lot to do with shame. I felt like a failure because my marriage didn't turn out to be the fairy tale that I had dreamed of. It was easier to pretend to the world that everything was perfect than to confess my dark secrets. Telling the truth would mean facing reality.

If I shared the problems with my family, then they would push me to make changes. They might question my judgment. Maybe they would doubt my ability to be a good mother because I chose to stay with a man who suffers from addiction. Then of course there was my fear that they would hate him. Even though I hated him much of the time myself, I wanted my family to love him. After all, I was holding out hope that he would get well and then nobody would ever need to know.

Eventually lying became second nature. The secrets had been kept for so long that the thought of opening up seemed overwhelming. Even when his addiction got bad enough that I couldn't hide it anymore, I still lied about how serious it was.

I didn't want to share the fact that I spent so much time crying that my eyes seemed to be permanently swollen. That my son barely talked to me anymore because he was so angry all of the time. That sometimes I slept in my car because I couldn't stand to be around Dean when he was high. Even if I did share those things, how could I explain why I was still with him? I couldn't even explain that to myself.

My fear caused me to close myself off from the rest of the world. It was easier to stay in my bubble of denial than to come out and face the unknown. As I worked on my inner strength, however, my fear began to fade. My self-esteem grew and as it did, I started to see things clearly.

I realized that by helping my husband keep his secret, I was enabling his disease. Even worse than that, I was teaching my son how to live in denial. I no longer wanted to live that way.

I had already changed my life in so many ways—I was taking care of myself by pampering, exercising, and eating healthfully; I had taken steps to further my career and financial future; I was getting in touch with my spirituality. Although I still held a huge fear of sharing the truth, I was finally feeling strong enough to move past that fear and reach out.

As soon as I turned to my family for help, a decade of baggage was lifted from my shoulders. It took all of my courage to make those first few phone calls, but my family rallied around me. They offered me so much love and support that for the first time in a long time, I felt protected.

They weren't judgmental, but they were firm. Their influence gave me the extra strength I needed to stand up to Dean's addiction and hold him accountable. I never understood how much power my secrets were holding over me until I let them go. By allowing myself to be vulnerable and open up, I was provided with the exact help I needed.

I now know that I wasn't only cheating myself by keeping a distance from my family, but I was cheating them as well. They wanted to be there for me. After all, helping to support each other is what family is all about.

Long ago families lived together, worked together, and built their lives around each other. That seems to have changed. We now tend to use our independence as an example of our strength. As we grow up, we grow away from our families, often limiting our connections to the occasional birthday party or holiday get-together. For some, needing help from your family has become a sign of weakness or failure.

You don't need to fall into that belief system. In your situation you need all the help and support that you can get. In many cases, your family is your biggest ally. Keep in mind that the word "family" can have a broad range of definitions. Maybe for you, your closest friends are your family. It doesn't have to be your mother, father, sister, or brother that you turn to for help. Look for the people in your life who have always been there for you and loved you unconditionally.

Only turn to those people you trust. Opening up does not mean that you have to share the truth with everybody in your life. You instinctively know who has your best interests at heart. You may be in the unfortunate situation of having nobody outside of your household that you can turn to. You are not alone. One of the best forms of support available, for those of us involved with an addict, is a family recovery group.

Al-Anon is the most popular family recovery group, but most cities have multiple groups to choose from, allowing each person to find the one that fits best. In these groups, the loved ones of addicts share their experience, struggles, and hope in order to gain strength and solve their common problems.

What better group of people to turn to for comfort and support than those who are living with the same struggles? It's important to understand, that if you're looking for a room full of people complaining about the addict, you will probably be disappointed. The focus is really not on the addict at all. The goal is to help loved ones with their own self-realization and growth.

The first time you walk into any type of family recovery meeting you might feel scared—but remember that everybody there understands. It doesn't matter who you are or where you come from—addiction causes the same feelings of shame, fear, anger, and hopelessness. I have found that regardless of which group I visit, I am welcomed with open arms by some of the most accepting people that I have ever met.

Many family recovery groups focus on a twelve step program. Through your participation you will be introduced to those twelve steps. This doesn't mean that you will be expected to follow some strict program. You decide for yourself which steps to tackle and what pace to go at.

For me the style of communication took some getting used to. At most of the groups I've visited, when one person is speaking there are no interruptions. That person is allowed to say everything that he or she wants to say before anybody else responds. I found this difficult at first—my natural style is to interject.

The first time I spoke at a meeting, I grew very emotional. I didn't expect so many feelings to come to the surface, but once I started talking, they just poured out of me. When I finished there was a long silence. It seemed like minutes went by before anyone else spoke. It was uncomfortable. I felt like running from the room. But then a woman sitting across from me opened up and shared her experience—which was so much like mine—and I immediately felt understood.

Although I was not used to this style of communication, I quickly realized how important it is for each person to be heard with no interruptions. I also got used to the occasional silence that happens. It takes time for people to gather their thoughts.

Don't worry if you have a fear of speaking in front of groups. There is usually no pressure to speak—especially as a newcomer. I never spoke during my first three or four meetings. It took me a while to feel comfortable enough to open up.

Aside from offering guidance and strength, most family recovery programs also encourage finding a mentor or sponsor—somebody who has been working the program for some time and can help you with daily struggles one-on-one. These are incredible support systems. In the case of Al-Anon, there are no dues or fees to join. Most groups pass around a basket for voluntary contributions so you can give whatever you can afford.

Visit a variety of groups in your area until you find the right one for you. Although the principles and goals are usually the same for most groups, there are differences. You might visit one group and find that they are mostly parents of children with addiction. Another group may only have families of alcoholics—if drugs are a factor in your situation you may feel more comfortable finding a group that can relate to the specific problems of drugs. It is perfectly fine, and encouraged, to keep looking until you find a group of people who resonate with you. There are even groups online.

Along with family recovery groups, there are countless other sources of support available. The most important thing is to break out of your isolation. Spending time outside of the addictive environment is crucial to your well being.

A support group can be any group of people that encourages your positive growth: an aerobics class, a reading group, your church—the list goes on and on. These people don't need to know every detail of your life in order to support your new path. Look for opportunities to spend time with people who are positive and leave you feeling good about yourself.

If you are uncomfortable being around groups of people, you may want to seek out a counselor so that you can gain guidance in a more intimate setting. If you have health coverage, check out what options are available. You may be eligible for counseling through your insurance. Just make sure that the counselor or therapist works with families of addicts on a regular basis. After all, the last thing you need is another person in your life who doesn't understand!

Some of the best guidance that I've received has been through books. Melody Beattie (*The Language of Letting Go*), Toby Rice Drews (*Getting Them Sober*), Wayne Dyer (*Manifest Your Destiny*), Shakti Gawain (*Meditations*), Depok Chopra (*The Seven Spiritual Laws of Success*), Sarah Ban Breathnach (*Simple Abundance*)—these authors and their writings helped to keep me on track. They were friends, teachers, and many times saviors.

I must admit that I have an addiction of my own—and that is books. They're stacked in every room of my house and I'm always in the process of reading several at a time. I personally prefer self-help and motivational writings. Every book that I bring home is like a little treasure of inspiration. I get excited about learning something new, gaining some new insight, or seeing things in a different light. Many of these books I've read several times over, and I always catch something new with each reading.

You might prefer fiction with its endless possibilities of romance, action, mystery, and suspense. These books can also be saviors. They have the power to pull you out of depression, take you to exotic lands, transport you back into time, send you off to another planet, and, most importantly, pull you away from your problems for a while.

In the addict household it's easy to become consumed with the addict. *What is he doing? What was he doing earlier? What is he going to do tomorrow? Should I be worried? I want to go out with my friends, but will he get into trouble while I'm gone? I'd better just stay home and keep an eye on him.* The family stops thinking about their own wants and needs while they make an attempt to control what the addict is doing. They are no longer living their own lives; instead, their world revolves around the addict. Because the world of addiction is crazy, the family's life becomes crazy.

That is why it's so important to pull yourself away from that chaos. Spending time with family and friends outside of your home, joining in on family recovery meetings, taking a class, going to church functions, losing yourself in a book for a while—these are all things that can bring some peace and balance into your life.

In your quest to find calm, be careful not to take an unhealthy route. The desire to escape your emotional pain can become so great that you may be tempted to reach out for any quick fix to find some relief.

None of us are immune to the grip of addiction. It can sneak up on you and take over before you realize what's happening. It looks for the right opportunity—when you're feeling weak and alone. It masks itself as a comforting friend. Only after it has seeped its way into every part of your life, plotting to destroy anything good or virtuous, do you start to see its true motives. But by then it has already sucked you deep into its spell.

I have watched several women that I know lose themselves to the same disease that they struggled to save their husbands from. It started with an innocent glass of wine in the evening to unwind from a hectic day, or a valium to ease the anxiety, but before they knew it, these seemingly innocent vices became crutches that they relied on.

It is devastating to a family when one member is struggling with addiction. But when both a husband and wife become addicts there is nothing more tragic. Who is left to care for the children? To give them hope? To be strong? It can't be left to the children to save their family. Don't take the chance of letting the very thing that is destroying your loved one get its hands on you.

Yes, one glass of wine may seem harmless. You're not the one with an addiction problem, after all. Why should you be cheated of this little pleasure? But how can you expect your loved one to stay abstinent if you can't deny these temptations yourself?'

Besides, that little glass of wine just becomes a big validation for the addict. "Why should you have a problem with my drinking?" he'll ask. "After all, you drink too." Never mind that it was the first drink that you've had in over six months and you didn't even finish the whole glass. He'll find a way to use it to justify his own actions. Why give him that ammunition?

Aside from drugs and alcohol, there are other destructive means of escape. Some of them start out as healthy habits that slowly transform into obsessions. Dieting and exercise are prime examples of this. I fell into this unhealthy pattern in my twenties.

At the time I was a stay-at-home mom and my husband was

already caught up in his addiction. Exercise was my release. It was my time to focus on myself and to escape my problems for a while. I would blast my favorite music and sweat out all of my cares. Afterward I would feel renewed.

But over time I started to get obsessed about my appearance. I wanted to have the perfect body and it became my mission. I was exercising for close to two hours every day while eating a very low calorie diet. At the time I was barely over one hundred pounds, but I would get bothered by the tiny pooch of fat on my lower belly or the small dimples on my butt. I was determined to exercise these imperfections away. I can remember working out for an hour, going to the mirror to study my naked body, and then, unhappy with my results, going back to complete another hour of exercise.

My family started to comment on how thin I was. I was suffering from headaches, catching a lot of colds, and my face was getting terrible break-outs. My body was obviously screaming out for me to stop this destructive pattern, but I refused to listen. It wasn't until I saw myself in a picture that reality hit. I looked so thin and sickly that I immediately started eating more and exercising less.

I can now look back over that time and clearly see that I was attempting to find some control in my life. Because I wasn't working, I had little control over my finances. I couldn't control my husband's addiction. My body was the one thing that I had complete control over. My initially healthy habits had turned into a disorder. Luckily I saw the light before it completely took over.

While over-exercising was my form of control for a while, the habit of overeating is more common. Food is an integral part of our lives. From the time we are infants, food is an expression of love. It is a huge part of our families and cultures. Certain foods can stir special memories or take us back to childhood. It is no surprise that most of us, at least on occasion, use food in order to comfort ourselves.

But in the addict household, the need for comfort is

frequent, so if food is your form of solace, you may find yourself with a damaging habit. Along with overeating comes weight gain, which usually results in lowered self-esteem. It then becomes a vicious cycle of eating to feel better—gaining weight from overeating—feeling depressed from the weight gain—and then eating more to temporarily feel better. We get stuck in this pattern because we are trying to fill a void deep inside of ourselves. The problem is that no amount of food will ever fill it up.

Some people use shopping in an attempt to fill this void. But just like food, while it may temporarily help you to feel better, the emptiness keeps coming back. I knew one woman who treated herself to a shopping spree every time her husband messed up. She decided that if he was going to throw away their money on drugs and alcohol, then she was going to get an equal amount of money to spend on whatever she wanted.

Of course, their bank account couldn't support this tit-for-tat attitude so she started opening up credit card accounts to finance all of the shopping. It didn't take long before the credit cards were all maxed out and they were in a deep financial hole.

When she talks about it now she can't believe how quickly she spent so much money. She also admits that it never brought her an ounce of joy—in fact, just the opposite. She became filled with guilt and shame, forced to hide merchandise and credit card statements in order to keep her secret. She had become a shopaholic, displaying many of the same addictive patterns as her husband.

The best way to stay out of these traps is by building your inner strength. The true friend deep inside of yourself is the strongest form of support that you can ever gain. It is through your inner strength that you will fill that void, that you will stop looking outside of yourself for comfort, and that you will finally come to realize that you are never alone.

It can be emotionally and physically exhausting when you're the only one in a relationship who is taking responsibility. The addict is like a spoiled adolescent. It is perfectly natural to get angry—and you need to allow yourself to get angry. It is normal to feel sorry for yourself—allow yourself to feel those emotions. But it is not okay to lose yourself in the same type of destructive habits as the addict.

Now is the time to reach out for help. If you can't find the courage to do that, then how can you expect the addict in your life to find the courage? Set the example and lead the way to positive change. Do it for your children. Do it for the addict. But especially do it for you.

Turn to the people who care about you and let them help to lift your load. Seek out and accept new friendships. Release the secrets that have been keeping you hostage. Honesty—not only with others but especially with yourself—is the key to freedom. Accept the fear of change and then take those first few steps out of the darkness and into your bright new future filled with family, friendships, and love.

Journaling Suggestion:

Write about your own negative habits. What means of escape do you use that don't support your positive new path? Do you have a few drinks when you're stressed? Do you smoke? Overeat? Shop when you can't afford it? Do you use TV as a form of escape? If you can't think of anything, then give yourself a week to monitor your own patterns. We get so used to focusing on the addict and all of his negative traits that we lose sight of our own challenges. Once you've discovered your own negative habit(s), set a goal to make a change. What new healthy habits will you take on to replace the old negative ones? Remember that you don't have to do this on your own. When you're lacking strength or faith you can borrow it. Pick up the phone and reach out to a friend. Join an Al-Anon group. Turn to family. By allowing people back into your life, you create a community of support and open the doorway to endless love.

*A real friend helps us think our best thoughts,
do our noblest deeds, be our finest selves.*
- Anon

I Am, I Have, I Feel

The mind is similar to a computer in the way that it's programmed. If your programming is healthy, it will reflect positively in your beliefs and how you function in this world. If your programming is somehow faulty, however, the negative effects will spread throughout every part of your life like a virus.

Your programming started from the moment you took your first breath. If you had loving parents, then you learned, even from infancy, that you were lovable. You saw the joy in their eyes when they looked at you. Their touches were warm and soft. You were well fed and taken care of. As a result you became secure. If, on the other hand, you had parents who were unable to give you the love that you required, you were programmed to believe that you were not lovable. Insecurity then takes root deep inside.

The programming continues on all throughout childhood. Your family, caretakers, teachers, and church all play a part. Even well-meaning parents can create negative programming without realizing the harm that they are causing. We tend to get labeled into certain roles from an early age, and then we follow suit.

Maybe you were the smart one growing up. You always

came home with A's on your report card and your parents would brag about how you would be the first one in your family to graduate from college. Your sister might have been the artistic one. She loved to draw, paint, and sculpt. Your parents would hang her art all around the home. It was clear who was good at what.

You may have had the desire to paint or draw, but that was not your role. You could never be as good at painting as your sister, so you never tried. Your sister may have stopped trying to get A's on her report card. Even if she got a couple of them she could never compete with the straight A's that you got. After all, you were the smart one and she was the artistic one. As a child you may have been labeled sensitive, hyperactive, fat, slow, loud, or a problem. These hurtful labels often follow you into adulthood.

Your parents may have taught you certain beliefs such as: money is scarce, men are more powerful than women, or it is selfish to think about yourself. Maybe you grew up with an abusive or addicted parent and you learned codependent behaviors at an early age. Because of that programming, you may have followed a certain path.

Even if your childhood was happy and healthy, bad programming can infect you later on. I was fortunate to be raised by loving parents who taught me to believe that I was smart, beautiful, and capable of anything. Was my household perfect? No—far from it. Were my parents without faults? Quite the opposite. But no matter what problems occurred, I always felt loved and secure.

After years of living with an addicted husband, however, my beliefs were affected. It didn't happen overnight. It was a gradual process that eventually left me feeling like a victim. In many ways I had become an empty shell, allowing the addiction to control my emotions, my actions, and my happiness. Affirmations helped to reverse that. It was an important step in a process that changed my life.

No matter what has happened to affect your beliefs and to

create your programming, you can change it. Just as you can upgrade your computer with new and better software, you can upgrade your mental software as well. By making a conscious effort to change your thoughts you begin to re-program your mind.

You repeat affirmations all day long whether you realize it or not. Every thought going through your head and every word that you say is an affirmation. Unfortunately, many of the thoughts and words that you affirm are likely negative. Complaining, whining, and worrying are all affirmations. In order to change your negative patterns you need to pay attention to your thoughts and words.

To become more aware of your current mental focus, ask yourself the following questions:

- What things do you tend to think about the most?

- Are there certain thoughts that keep you up at night?

- Are you more aware of what you have or what you are lacking?

- What habits do you have?

- How much time do you spend thinking about each of these habits?

- Do your thoughts tend to focus more on the negative or the positive?

Use your answers to these questions as a guideline for where you may need to make some changes. While it would be impossible to control every thought that enters your mind, you do have control over your thinking. You choose whether to think positively or negatively. You decide whether to see the glass as half-full or half-empty. You make the choice whether to stay angry or to forgive.

Most of us were never taught that we have control over our thinking. We go through our lives believing that our thoughts and feelings are just a result of what is happening around us. We assume that they are an automatic response.

As I learned how to use affirmations I came to understand that my thoughts and feelings belonged to me. In the past I would blame my husband, or whatever situation was occurring, for any bad feelings that I had. It wasn't my fault that I was filled with rage or sadness. I felt that way because of him. I couldn't help it. He was the one causing me to be depressed, resentful, or hopeless. But then I learned how to turn my thinking around.

No person, situation, or problem has any power over your own thoughts unless you hand that power over. This is also why you have no control over anyone else. You cannot manipulate another person to become what you want them to be, or to feel the way you want them to feel. Sometimes your manipulations may work because the other person allows it, but you should not waste any of your own energy on attempting to control others.

I have found that the best way to take control of my thoughts and feelings is to stay focused on the present moment. Most negative thoughts are based on either the past or the future. We all know that you can't change the past, so when you find yourself stuck in hurtful memories, you can give yourself a reminder to return to the present. Get out of your head and give your full attention to whatever you are doing. Focus on your work, or the conversation that you are sharing, or whatever task or pleasure is right in front of you.

The same goes for those times when you find yourself worrying about the future. The past is gone and the future does not exist. This moment is all that you have. If you can think happy thoughts right in this moment, then you are living a happy life.

Staying in the present moment is not easy for most of us. It seems to be the habit of the mind to wander off anywhere but the present. It can help to do a quick centering exercise throughout the day. It only takes a few seconds. Whenever you find your mind consumed by chaotic thoughts, take a deep breath and listen to any sounds going on around you. Just listen. This will help to quiet your mind. Now focus on whatever feeling is happening inside of you. If it feels anything but good, then it's time to change your thoughts.

What are the thoughts that create happiness for you? Keep those on file for when you need them. As you come across new thoughts that bring you joy, or make you feel warm and fuzzy, you can add them to your reserve.

I have several that always work for me. I like to imagine being at my favorite vacation spot—San Diego. Thinking about the long walks on the beach, the sun against my skin, and listening to the waves has an immediate calming effect for me. I can picture my dog Molly when she first wakes and looks up at me with her tired and wrinkled face—just thinking about her makes me smile. If a specific person or problem is bothering me, it helps to imagine blowing that problem into a balloon and then releasing it. As I imagine it floating away, the negative feelings tend to lift away with it.

If you find yourself stuck in sadness, anger, resentment, or regret because of the past then you must find a way to let it go. Otherwise you will allow the past to hold you back from happiness now and in the future. If you are having a difficult time detaching from those negative feelings, you may have some forgiveness to work on. Remember that forgiveness has little to do with the other person. You are not condoning their behavior. Forgiveness is releasing the negative emotions that are only hurting you.

This all comes down to being aware of your own thoughts and feelings. This is the key to changing your life. Your thoughts are powerful. As you start to use affirmations on a regular basis, you reverse the negative habits of the mind.

In order for affirmations to to be the most effective, you should believe in the possibility of what you are affirming. This is why negative affirmations tend to work so well. When you repeat over and over that life is hard, it's easy to find the evidence of that. When you first learn to use positive affirmations, however, you may have a difficult time believing in what you are affirming.

You may repeat the words, "My success comes easily and effortlessly," but your deeper thoughts may be saying, "Yeah, right—life is hard work". You can continue to repeat your new positive affirmation over and over again for weeks, but if your belief is still that life is hard work, then hard work is likely the result that you will get.

There might be negative beliefs that have been with you for many years, maybe your entire life. Expecting to change those beliefs overnight would be unrealistic. But the mind is incredibly resilient. The trick is to start changing those habitual beliefs by changing your thinking. If you can begin to think more positive thoughts than negative ones, the scale will eventually tip in your favor.

It's important to understand that whatever you focus on will be what you create in your life. For example, if you are in credit card debt and you find yourself constantly worrying about bills and debt, you will probably find that bills and debt continue to pile up faster than you can keep up. That is because your focus is on just that—bills and debt. Without realizing it, you are affirming that what you want is more bills and debt because that is your focus.

If instead you started repeating an affirmation such as, *I have more than enough money for everything that I want and need,* you start to re-focus in a positive direction. Simply repeating your affirmation is not enough though. As you say the words, you need to get into that frame of mind. Imagine what it would feel like to open the mailbox each day knowing that there will be no collection notices. Knowing that you have more than enough money to pay all of your bills and that you are financially secure. Hold that feeling as you repeat your affirmation.

Look at the areas of your life in which you are unsatisfied. What beliefs do you have about these areas that may be holding you back from happiness? Do you long for a loving and trusting marriage, but believe that relationships like that are only in fairy tales? Is your dream to live in a gorgeous home on the beach, but you can't even fathom ever having enough money to live that way?

If you could have anything in life that you want, what would it be? This is the question that you should ask yourself. You only get one shot to live this life, so don't put limitations on your dreams.

Do some soul-searching to figure out what your true desires are. What changes do you want to make in your life? This is not about the addict. You may want him to change, but you can't control that. Instead, focus on the changes that you want to make in your own life.

The next step is to come up with some specific affirmations that will help to change any negative beliefs that are holding you back. Here are some guidelines to follow when designing your affirmations:

- They should be written and spoken in the present tense, *I am, I have, or I feel.* If you use words that express that you are hoping for something, or that something is on its way, then you are only creating more hoping and waiting.

- Keep them positive. For example, don't say, *I am no longer tired all of the time.* Instead say, *I am full of vibrant energy all day long.*

- Focus on yourself. You cannot use affirmations to control others.

- It can be helpful to create an affirmation rhyme or jingle. This makes it attractive to your mind.

- It's good to say your affirmations out loud as often as you can. This helps to give them a strong voice.

- Have faith in your affirmations. You can only achieve your desires once you believe that they are possible.

By repeating your new positive affirmations throughout the day, you are teaching your mind new self-talk. The mind likes to repeat things. The good news is that you have control over what it repeats.

Once I started using affirmations as a daily practice, I began catching my mind using them when I wasn't even trying. I'd be driving to work, or blow-drying my hair, or doing the dishes, and suddenly I would notice that my mind was repeating a little affirmation song that I had made up: *I am healthy, I am strong, I am happy all day long.*

I would feel so proud—like the pride that a mom feels when she catches her child doing something good. I realized that I was reprogramming my mind. In the past, it would go off on its own tangents (usually negative), but I was now teaching it a much healthier habit.

Make affirmations a part of your daily ritual. Incorporate them into your normal routine and eventually your mind will automatically repeat your affirmations without a lot of effort on your part. For example, I have several times during the day that I repeat my affirmations: in the shower, when I'm putting on my makeup, and while I'm on my evening walk. I picked these times because I found that these were the moments that my mind seemed to wander the most. By refocusing my mind during these tasks, I have reversed much of my negative thinking.

Now when I turn on the shower, my mind automatically starts repeating my affirmations. It has become a part of that routine, the same as shampooing my hair. There are occasional days that it doesn't happen automatically. I'll catch my mind having some sort of jumbled thoughts. At that time I quickly change my thinking and jump into my affirmations. The wonderful thing is that I am now aware of what's going on in my mind and I've learned to take control of it.

Some people go on spiritual journeys in order to find themselves. I personally believe that life is not about finding yourself; instead, I believe that life is about creating yourself.

You have the power to decide who you are and what you do in this life. If you don't like the direction you're going, you can change it. You can reinvent yourself anytime you like.

With an open mind and heart, take a close look at the life that you are leading now. Keep doing the things that bring you happiness. Hold on to those qualities that make you special. You can let go of everything else. If you have habits that leave you feeling badly, you can break them. If you have personality traits that you don't like, then you can change them. It's never too late to start anew.

What kind of life do you want to lead from here on out? What changes need to be made to create that life? Now design the affirmations that will keep you focused on those changes. It is a good idea to have an affirmation for each area of your life; personal, financial, and spiritual. Following are some of my favorite affirmations. Pick the ones that speak to you, or make up your own.

Every cell of my body is healthy and strong.
I am physically fit and I love the way my body looks and feels.
I nourish my body with healthy foods and it rewards me.
I am full of vibrant energy all day long.
I am living in my dream home.
I have more than enough money for everything that I need.
I attract prosperity like a magnet.
Opportunity opens the door in every direction that I turn.
I love the work that I do and I am paid abundantly for it.
I am financially secure.
My success comes easily.
I am surrounded by supportive family and friends.
I attract healthy relationships into my life.
I am surrounded by love.
I accept only good into my life.

I have plenty of extra time for rest and play.
Today I listen to my inner guide and it tells me everything
that I need to know.
Today I release the past with love.
My life is filled with joy and I am so grateful.
I am surrounded by beauty.
I love myself exactly the way that I am.
I am healthy, I am strong, I am happy all day long.
I love my life.

After you repeat your affirmations, imagine releasing them out into the universe. Know that you will be rewarded for your positive thinking. Don't get caught up in worrying about how long it will take. Have faith that everything will unfold at the perfect time.

Continue to move in the right direction with confidence. You are planting the seeds of your future. By keeping the soil nourished (positive thinking); you are creating a healthy environment for the blooms of your future to thrive.

I once planted tulip bulbs in my garden. I followed all of the proper steps: I first refrigerated the bulbs, then I planted them in the right month at the proper depth, and I made sure to keep them watered and well protected. But as the weeks went by and my bulbs weren't sprouting, I became anxious. What if I did something wrong and my tulip bulbs were dead? I got so frustrated wondering and waiting that I went out and dug up a section. I found that the green stems were just getting ready to break through the surface. Excited, I gently covered them back up and left them alone.

A few days later the ground was covered with pointy green stems shooting up toward the sun. Except that is, for the spot that I had disturbed. Saddened that I may have hurt those bulbs, I kept the area watered and protected. But as the patch of thriving tulips came to bloom, the disturbed area made no change.

Digging up the section again, I discovered that the green stems that had once been growing from the bulbs were now gone. My inability to have faith that my tulips were on their way, caused me to destroy their fertile home. As a result they failed to survive.

So it is with your affirmations. Keep your mind nourished with healthy thinking. Continue taking steps in the right direction. And most importantly, have faith that the seeds of your future are growing strong. One day you will wake up and be surrounded by the beautiful blooms of happiness that the power of your positive thinking helped to create.

Journaling Suggestion:

In your journal, list three affirmations that you will focus on. Then make a commitment to repeat these affirmations at a specific time each day. For example, you could choose to repeat your affirmations every time that you brush your teeth. If you spend three minutes brushing your teeth (which, by the way, is the amount of time my dentist recommends), and you brush your teeth at least twice a day, you will be repeating your affirmations for six minutes every day. But chances are that your mind will latch onto your new affirmations like much-needed nourishment. Before you know it, you will probably find yourself repeating your affirmations all throughout the day. Don't forget to release your affirmations out into the universe and keep the faith.

Every thought that we think is creating our future.
-Louise L. Hay

See It, Believe It

While affirmations are a step to changing your thoughts and beliefs, visualization is the key to creating a clear blueprint for your mind. Once you have a well-defined vision, it is easier to manifest what you want from life. Your subconscious mind does not differentiate between the real world and your vivid imagination. It responds equally to each. As you fully experience your desires through visualization, your subconscious mind will deposit these as truths. What your subconscious mind believes to be true is what you will ultimately see as your reality.

The method of visualization has been proven to work. In the world of sports, Olympic and professional athletes have been using visualization for decades. One of the best known studies on the effects of visualization in sports was conducted in Russia. Scientists compared four groups of Olympic athletes. The first group focused one-hundred percent on physical training. The second group focused seventy-five percent on physical and twenty-five percent on mental training. The third group focused fifty percent on each. The fourth group focused twenty-five percent on physical and seventy-five percent on mental training. They found that group four, the group that spent the most time on mental training, performed the best.

Exercises of visualization or guided imagery are also widely used in the field of medicine. When I first started to learn about visualization, I read several books and articles that talked about the effects that it had on a variety of health issues including pain management, weight loss, and chronic disease. In some cases, patients seemed to recover from untreatable cancers by using visualization techniques. The patients would spend time picturing their healthy immune cells destroying their bad cancer cells. They each pictured their good immune cells differently; some pictured them as knights on horseback attacking the weaker cancer cells, some as dogs eating them up like pieces of meat. What the specific image was didn't seem to matter as much as the frequency of practice and the enthusiasm involved.

The power that visualization proved to have over health issues intrigued me, and I decided to test it out on myself. While I was fortunate to be free of any serious health conditions, I did have a wart on my right index finger that had been bothering me. I decided that I would use the imaging technique that the cancer patients used to attack the wart. I had read that many cancer patients use white polar bears in their imaging because they represent health. So I chose the white polar bear as my hero.

Each night before going to sleep, I would visualize a group of white polar bears making the trip up my arm, to my hand, eventually finding the wart on my finger. I would then picture them devouring the wart until it was all gone. After that they would rub their bellies with contentment, smile at me, and make their way back home (they seemed to reside somewhere under my bed).

I continued to do this for about two weeks, but eventually lost interest in it. A few days later I was doing some yard work and rubbed my finger up against something. I noticed a small object flick away from my finger. I looked down, and to my amazement, the wart was gone. It had simply fallen off. To this day I still have a small white spot where the wart was, but it has never come back. I have no doubt that it was the imagery of white polar bears that conquered my wart.

Witnessing the result of visualization, I began to use it more and more, and as I did a new world opened up to me. It goes far beyond sports and health. No matter what desires you have, and no matter what is going on in your life, visualization is a tool that can positively affect you.

I love a story that my sister Leah tells about the proof of visualization. One day she was waiting to meet with a client who was known to be a real brute. She was worried about the outcome of the meeting because he was already upset about some issues and she wasn't looking forward to being on the receiving end of his negativity. As she sat in the waiting area of his office, she decided to picture a halo over her head. She thought that if he could see her as an angel it would be difficult to give her a hard time. As she sat there picturing her halo the receptionist glanced her way, "You look just like a little angel sitting there." she said to Leah. Astounded at the instant power of her visualization, Leah beamed inside. She continued picturing the halo, confident that her client would see the same. Well, the meeting did go wonderfully well and it was obvious that her client couldn't help but adore her.

You can use visualization to improve every aspect of your life, from gaining confidence for an interview to obtaining the home that you've always wanted. By creating a clear image in the mind, you set forth the energy needed to bring your dreams to life. Of course, the bigger the desire, the more time and energy it will take before it's realized, but tapping into the power of your mind is the key to reaching your desires, no matter how distant they seem.

Your most powerful tool is your imagination, and visualization is simply focused imagination. Every time you think about something your mind creates a picture or a sensory response. For example, when you get ready to make yourself a sandwich, you first see or taste or feel the sandwich in your mind. If you're really hungry, your mouth may even water at the thought of your sandwich. When you are thinking about a situation, you play it out in your mind just like a movie. We all daydream, but we have the ability to guide those daydreams into positive images that can enhance our lives.

Most daydreams tend to wander from one topic to the next with little or no control. Much of the time they are focusing on anything and everything that could possibly go wrong. As you worry, your mind creates the pictures that go along with those concerns. *The economy is so bad right now.* You worry. *What if I lose my job?* And along with that thought comes a picture. You see yourself unable to feed your family, losing your home, and fear sets in. By focusing on poverty, you are opening the doorway to allow poverty into your life.

If, on the other hand, you make a conscious effort to use your imagination to guide your life in a positive direction, you can tap into unlimited potential. The first step is to have a clear intention.

What do you want? What would make you happy? Pick the things that you have control over. Once you've figured it out take a closer look. For example, almost all of us wish for more money in our lives. But is it really money that we want? Is it green paper tucked away in a bank that we long for? No. It is the security, or the freedom, or the lavish lifestyle that the money could buy. So before you start using visualization to create what you want, make sure to narrow it down to your truest desires.

Now that you have decided on an intention, your mind can start to focus on your desired outcome. It knows what you want so it can work on your behalf. Your job is to see your vision, have faith, and move in the direction of your dreams. It is natural for some doubt to creep in, but as those uncertainties arrive, quickly show them out.

Create a vivid image in your mind of what you want. The more that you get your senses involved the better. For example, if your desire is to get into shape, see yourself looking great in a sexy bikini. Notice how toned your muscles are. Imagine touching your skin and feeling how tight and smooth your skin feels. Take notice of your natural energy and enthusiasm. You might picture yourself walking along a beach. Smell the ocean air. Feel the warmth of the sun against your skin. Enjoy the feeling of pride and self-confidence that you now exude.

Visualization is a skill that can be mastered. Like any skill, you get better with practice. Some people have an easier time using their imagination than others. I am one of those fortunate ones. I've always had an active imagination. As a little girl I was constantly dreaming up my own world. Sometimes my backyard was a giant city with castles and dragons and moats. Other times it was a futuristic world filled with flying saucers and robots. But never was it simply a backyard. In my mind it was always something magical.

Dolls and stuffed animals weren't just toys, they were truly alive. I had one doll, Beth, whom I took care of for several years. I fed her, and dressed her, and loved her every day until one day when my sister came into my room and hit me with a dose of reality. "You know," she said, "You're getting ready to start junior high so you can't play with dolls anymore." As much as it hurt to hear those words, I knew that she was right. That week I prepared Beth for the inevitable. I explained as best I could why I would no longer be able to care for her. It was heartbreaking, but at the end of the week I tucked Beth into my closet and never played with her again.

After that day, I stopped fostering my imagination. It was still a part of me but I attempted to shut it off. Then when I became a mother I got the chance to bring it back. My son inherited the same active imagination and it was great fun joining him in his adventures. Once again stuffed animals and dolls came to life. I can remember tucking him into bed at night and all of his toys would speak to me. "Put me next to him," his monkey would cry. "No, it's my turn," I'd hear his Ninja Turtle yell. So I'd attempt to make all of his toys happy and tuck them close to Jesse.

My son is all grown up now, but my imagination is still strong. Just recently, I caught myself talking to toys again. I am a retail manager and I was packing up all of the teddy bears after the Christmas season was over. As I put them into the box, I heard one of them crying, "Hey, I can't breathe down here." So I reached down and pulled his head up so that he wouldn't suffocate. Then I could hear another shouting, "What about me?" So down I reached to pull that one up. One by one, I situated all the bears so that they were comfortable. "Don't worry," I told them as I shut the box, "It's only for a little while." Of course, I told them this telepathically—God forbid one of my employees would walk in and see me talking to stuffed animals!

The good thing about having such an active imagination is that it makes it easy for me to visualize. You may not use your imagination very often. Maybe you remember using it a lot as a child but now you don't know whether you can get it back. Fortunately, imagination is something that we all have, and you can always wake it up. If you were asked to describe your home, you would immediately retrieve a picture in your mind. From memory alone you would see the furniture, the color of the walls, the carpet or tile, and you would be able to describe it. This is all the imagination it takes to visualize.

We use our memories to retrieve pictures all the time. The difference with visualization is that you create the pictures you want instead of relying on memory alone. You are not limited to any rules. You are free to design anything you wish. The process can be a lot of fun, but just because it's fun doesn't mean it's a silly game. It is a proven way to get the cooperation of your mind.

In the time that I have been using visualization, I have witnessed remarkable changes in my life. I have gone from being in a marriage with an out-of-control addict to now being in a supportive relationship with the same man. Just over five years ago, I had lost practically all of my possessions. My house was empty—after I moved out of our home, Dean traded almost every piece of furniture and electronics for drugs—and we were on the verge of foreclosure. Now we've accumulated all new possessions and our home is just a couple of years away from being paid off. Dean and I have purchased two pieces of property, one in our current state of Arizona and one in the beautiful mountains of New Mexico, to build our dream home and dream vacation home. I've been promoted three times in those five years and now have a top management position making five times the salary that I was making to start. Most importantly, I am no longer the scared and depressed person that I was back then. Instead I feel positive and confident. I look back and clearly see the evidence that visualization works.

One of the greatest benefits to using visualization is the awareness of control that it offers you. Being in a relationship with an addict can leave you feeling powerless. By learning to use the tools of visualization, you start to feel a sense of mastery over your own life, which in turn increases your self-esteem and hopefulness for the future.

The biggest challenge can be keeping your passion on the right focus. When you love a person with an addiction, you can grow very passionate with contempt and fear. It's difficult to turn your attention away from the addict and his problems. You must understand that the stronger emotions and the stronger visions hold the power. For that reason, you must find a way to turn your passion over to your dreams rather than keeping it directed on your problems.

Practice makes perfect. It doesn't happen overnight. A lot has happened to create your current mindset, but through regular practice of visualization, you can change it. As your positive visions of the future grow clear and strong, your passion will evolve. You will free yourself from the trap of fear and look towards your promising future.

Make it a point to take at least one step every day toward your vision. No matter how small the step might be, it's important to keep moving toward it. If your vision is to be a nurse, but you still need to get your nursing degree, then a step might be calling your local college to speak with a guidance counselor. If your vision is to be in shape, but you are currently thirty pounds overweight, then your step today might be sticking to your diet.

Don't get overwhelmed by the big picture, simply take it one step at a time. Keep your vision clear in your mind and before you know it, you'll be looking back, amazed at how far you've come.

I've read books that lead you to believe that visualizing is the only step that you need to take in order to create the life of your dreams. You're left with the idea that as long as you clearly hold your vision in your mind, it will eventually appear in your life like magic. But this belief can only set you up for failure. I challenge you to find any person living their dream who didn't take physical steps toward their goals. Even to win the lottery, you must physically go to the store and purchase a ticket.

If you want to be a bodybuilder, then you must lift weights. If you want to be a writer, then you must put words to paper. If you want a promotion, you wouldn't call in sick every day so that you could spend those eight hours visualizing the promotion. If you did you would certainly be fired. Taking the steps required to reach your goals is what makes the difference between manifesting and simply dreaming.

So then why visualize at all? Because once you have the support of your mind, nothing can get in your way. Having a clear vision creates the confidence, focus, and energy required to achieve your dreams. It's like having the map that will lead you to the buried treasure. Once your mind knows what you want, it will help to guide you in the right direction.

Just recently I was watching an interview with Jim Carey, who shared his story of manifesting. Long before he became one of the most highly-paid entertainers in the industry, he walked up to the Hollywood Hills and wrote himself a check for ten million dollars. On the memo line he wrote, *for services rendered.* He carried the check around with him for years, confident that he would eventually be paid that kind of money. It was a bigger dream than most people ever dare to imagine, but it did manifest, and now he is paid twice as much as that for a film. Did he succeed because of the check that he wrote? No. But the check did serve a purpose. It was a constant reminder of his goals. And I would bet that any time he felt like giving up, all he had to do was look at that check and it gave him the push he needed to keep going.

Don't be afraid of dreaming big. Just because it might seem like a long distance from where you are right now, don't use your current circumstances as an excuse to settle for less. You have the power within you to change everything. Don't let fear put limitations on your dreams.

You could choose to play it safe. You might decide that your big dream is to hike up a hill. All you need for the trip is protective shoes and some water. This is a goal that you can easily reach, so you aren't setting yourself up for disappointment. When you reach the top of the hill, you might feel good about your accomplishment, but you will probably never make it any further than that hill.

On the other hand, after doing some soul-searching, you may realize that your big dream is to shoot for the stars. You know that it won't be easy. There will probably be a lot of turbulence along the way. The people around you may scoff at your plans. "You'll never make it that far," they protest. But you know that it's what you want, so you go for it despite their warnings.

There's no reason to be afraid. What's the worst that can happen? Maybe you don't reach the stars, but instead only make it to the moon. A trip to the moon is nothing to laugh at. I don't know about you, but I'd much rather look back over my life and know that I took a chance and made it to the moon, instead of staying safe and only making it to the top of some hill.

Don't get me wrong—the top of a hill is great if that's what you truly want and what will truly make you happy. Your dreams don't have to be big—just genuine. You deserve to have everything that you want in this life, and it can be yours. The first step is to believe.

Journaling Suggestion:

The following exercise will help you to discover what your true dream is. Many times what we think is our dream is quite different if we look more deeply at our desires. By asking yourself *why* you want something, you can gain insight into what would truly make you happy. Here is an example:

What is your dream?
My dream is to win a million dollars in the lottery.

Why would winning a million dollars make you happy?
Because then I could quit my job.

Why would quitting your job make you happy?
Because I wouldn't have to answer to a boss anymore and I would have lots of free time.

What would you do with all of your free time?
I would pursue my passion of photography.

So looking at your answers, what is your true dream?
To become a great photographer so that I can make a living doing what I love and no longer work for somebody else.

Now state your dream as an affirmation.
I am a successful freelance photographer making enough money to support my family and have everything that I want and need.

Now it's your turn...

All that we are is a result of what we have thought.
The mind is everything. What we think, we become.
-Buddha

Creating a Clear Vision

There are many techniques that you can use to create a clear vision of your intention. It can be helpful to try some of the following methods in order to clarify the details of your vision. This is where the fun comes in. Pick one or two to try, or do what I do and dabble in all of them. The more involved you get in your vision, the faster your manifestation will occur.

Dream List

I would suggest having a separate journal or notebook in which to keep your dream list. This will be an ongoing project for you. Start off by writing a special phrase or affirmation that sums up your overall desires. This will be your motto or mission statement. Mine, for example, is *Every Day is a New Opportunity for Joy, Fun, and Success. I Love My Life and I Am So Grateful!* Having a mission statement for your life makes every decision easier. You simply need to ask, "Does this move me towards my mission?"

Now you can start your list. Be sure to phrase each item as if you have already received it. So if you want a new car, you would write *I have a new car.* Better yet, *I have a new red convertible Corvette* (or whichever car you dream of having).

Keep listing all the items that you can think of. Write down the things that you want to own, big and small—from a new cocktail dress to a beach house. Write down the goals that you want to achieve. You should even write down the way that you want to feel. As new desires arrive you will add these to your list.

Because you are writing in the present tense, you are creating affirmations. Make it a regular practice to read through your list. As you read each affirmation, take a moment to clearly picture the end result in your mind. So if an item on your list is *I enjoy spending lots of quality time with family and friends,* picture what that looks like to you. Maybe it's enjoying a Sunday dinner with all of the people you love. Imagine how delicious the air smells. Feel how relaxed and joyful you are. Notice the smiles and laughter that surround you. You might want to picture your loved one at that table—looking happy and healthy. Just because you can't use visualization to change another person doesn't mean that you can't include their sobriety in your dreams of the future.

Once you have that picture clear in your mind, move on to the next item on your list. Some items will be quick and easy to visualize, such as a new pair of tennis shoes. Others might take a bit more effort. Remember, the more vivid the details of your visualizations, the more cooperation you will receive from your mind. When you are done going over your list, imagine all of them combining into a big bubble of bright light and then release the bubble out into the universe.

Over time you will notice that there are items on your list that have manifested. Do something special to celebrate those achievements. I also like to go over those items with a highlighter. Opening up my journal and seeing those highlighted items serves as a reminder that I control my own destiny.

There is power in the written word. People who make a habit of writing down their goals know this. It takes the vague foggy ideas that may be lingering in the back of your mind and turns them into clear intentions.

Suzie Orman, the financial expert and best-selling author, has told the story of how she used the written word to help create her dream. She had just landed a job at Merrill Lynch, but she was terrified that she wouldn't succeed at meeting her sales quota. Every morning before she went to work she would write: *I am young, powerful, and successful, producing at least $10,000 a month.* Well, she definitely reached her target goal and has now far surpassed it. She believes that writing down her goal each day helped to make it materialize.

Dream Story

For this exercise, you will be writing a short story detailing your perfect day. In your story you will want to combine all of your big desires. So if your goals are to be in shape, have a home by a lake, and have a fulfilling career, then all of those aspects should be included in your story.

Before you start this project you will want to clear your mind. If you've had an active day it might be a good idea to take a warm bath in order to relax. Put on something comfortable and find a spot where you will be left alone. Now get ready to let your imagination go. There is no right or wrong way to write your story. You will not be graded on spelling and grammar. This is only for you, so have fun with it!

Your story should start from the moment you open your eyes. What do you see? How do you feel? Where are you? Now keep going from there. Allow yourself to escape into your dream world and write down every detail. You will want to include not only the physical details, but the emotional as well. Are you feeling confident? Do you laugh a lot? Are you completely in love? What is it about this new life that makes you so happy? Keep moving through the entire day and then give it a perfect ending.

When you are finished, take a break and then come back a little while later to read your story. This exercise can be especially helpful if you have difficulty with the idea of visualizing. When you read or hear a story, you see the images of that story in your mind. This is something that you have been doing since you were a child.

Now that you have written and read your story, it has become a part of your consciousness. It has been registered into your memory just like every other book or story that you have read. What's different about this story is that you are the main character and you have now gotten a glimpse of the extraordinary life that awaits you.

From now on, whenever you think about or read your story, know that it's becoming a reality. Have confidence that your future is already being prepared for you because you are taking an active role in creating it. Everything that happens in your life starts with a thought. You think about getting out of bed and then you really do get out of bed. You think about going to work and then you really do go to work. You think about making a bowl of ice cream with sliced bananas and chocolate syrup and then you really do make a bowl of ice cream with sliced bananas and chocolate syrup. This is no different. It may just take more time because the idea is bigger. But as long as you keep your focus on your dream, and remain confident that it's on its way, you will eventually find yourself living the life that you created in your story.

Keep in mind that you can create as many stories as you like. There are many days in your future, not just one. So if you enjoy this project do it again and again. You are a creator and what better thing to create than your future.

Dream Board

Creating a dream board is a great outlet for your artistic side. But even if you think you don't have an artistic bone in your body, you will have fun with this project. If you have children, this can be a wonderful way to spend time together. They can create their own dream boards and you will be teaching them the tools of visualization.

You are the designer of your life, so the idea here is to do what designers do. When an interior designer is coming up with the plans to redecorate a room, she collects swatches of fabric, paint samples, pictures of furniture and art, and then she will typically put them all together into a presentation. This allows her clients to clearly see her vision. With a dream board, you are going to create a collage that represents your own vision.

The first step is deciding on your theme. You can keep your dream board focused on just one area of your life, for example your dream home, or your dream career, or maybe having a healthy lifestyle and being fit. Or you might decide to incorporate all of your future aspirations to create a collage of your dream life one year, or three years, or five years from now.

The second step is to collect the materials for your collage. You can attempt to do this all in one day, but you may have a difficult time finding the right pictures and materials to create an authentic dream board in such a short time. Instead, I recommend making this collecting phase a process of days or even weeks, looking for just the right pictures that reflect your truest desires. Once you have collected enough items then you can plan some time to put it all together.

During this collecting phase you will gather pictures, words, and phrases from various sources including magazines, brochures, catalogs, the internet, and even your own personal collection of postcards and pictures. The purpose is to find those images that represent the life experience you wish to create. It isn't just about the things that you want to acquire, it's much more about the lifestyle that you want to lead.

When you are ready to put your dream board together, you will want a blank canvas to work with. A large piece of poster board works perfectly and is quite inexpensive. You will also need scissors and glue (I prefer a glue stick). There may be other items that you want to include such as glitter, colorful markers, beads, sea shells—the sky's the limit. You are free to get as creative and artistic as you like.

You are the visionary in this process, so the only right way to design your dream board is your own way. You may prefer to keep things organized with straight lines and borders. Or you might like things more abstract, cutting your pictures into odd shapes and sizes, feeling free to randomly apply the pictures without over-thinking the process. I would suggest, however, laying out your pictures first before finalizing your design with glue.

Once your dream board is complete, spend some time admiring your work of art. You may see some new things that you didn't notice while you were in the process. Let your collage speak to you. Then make sure to hang or set it in a spot where you will see it on a regular basis.

Your dream board is a visual affirmation. By looking at it regularly you are imprinting those images clearly in your mind. In a short time you will no longer need to look at your dream board in order to see those images. They will be vivid in your memory and follow you wherever you go.

Dream Book

A dream book is really the same concept as a dream board only the format is different. A photo album or scrap book works perfectly. The nice thing about a photo album is that you don't have to glue the pictures down, so you can move them around or easily remove a picture if your vision changes. I personally like to make duplicate copies of the pictures that mean a lot to me; that way I can include them in multiple collages and books.

The benefit to having a dream book is that it can easily travel with you. I like to keep mine in my car: that way if I get stuck in a traffic jam, instead of frustration building up, I can open up my dream book and be transformed into my vision.

I currently have a dream book for my future dream home. Because Dean and I have already purchased the property for this home, one of our favorite things to do is take a weekend drive to go plan and dream at this location.

I already have the home design picked out, the landscaping ideas, the style of furniture, the colors for the walls, the type of appliances—you name it and I already have it clear in my mind and in my book. As we travel to our property, I take with me my dream book for that home. When we pull up I don't see an empty piece of land. I see the driveway, the walkway to the front door, the porch, the walls, and everything else that makes it real. To me it's as though this home already exists on some level—it's just a matter of time before the rest of the world sees it.

Dream Box

My mother got me started on my first dream box. Years ago I went to her home and she pulled out her dream box to show me. She had taken a beautiful fabric-covered shoe box and inside was a treasure of pictures representing the life of her dreams. Each picture was perfectly mounted on a colorful index card. Along the borders she wrote phrases and affirmations that went along with the pictures. I was so inspired to start my own dream box that I went straight from her home to the art supply store to get the items I needed.

Did you have a hope chest when you were younger? I never did, but I always wanted one. Now I have my dream box and it's so much better than a hope chest, because it holds things far bigger than fine linens. It can house big dreams like a trip to Hawaii, a new career, or a fulfilling marriage.

Whether you create a dream board, dream book, dream box, write your dream story, or come up with your own ideas, I encourage you to experiment with this type of visioning. Not only is it fun, but it helps to keep your energy focused on those positive desires. By concentrating on your dreams, you help to magnetize them to you.

The science of quantum physics has proven that everything, including each one of us, is made up of energy. At our cores, beyond our skin, bones, organs, molecules, and atoms, that is what we are. It has also shown that like energy attracts like energy. So if you focus on the negative, then that is what you will attract toward you. If you focus on the positive, then more positive things will come your way.

Starting today see yourself as you are—a magnet. Make a conscious effort to only attract into your life those things that you want. Focus on the positive. Clearly see your dreams. Close the door to negative thoughts. When you catch them creeping in, push them back out. In this way, you truly have control over your life and future.

Journaling Suggestion:

Write a clear description of the lifestyle that you want. Be precise in expressing the details. Create a visualization on paper, much like a playwright would describe a scene. By doing this you are not only defining your desires, but rehearsing what life will be like once they are attained. Writing down your dreams is one way of stating that you believe they're achievable. It is the first step in committing to your goals. Then take steps every day to reach them. Before you know it, these steps (however small) will add up to a long distance. You'll look back at how far you've come and the excitement will create a momentum that pushes you the rest of the way.

Shoot for the moon, even if you miss it
you will land among the stars.
-Les Brown

The Path of Recovery

How can he be so selfish? He can clearly see how much pain he's causing—why doesn't he care? I can't take the stress any longer. He's destroying all of our dreams. Our lives have become Hell. Isn't he tired of living this way?

These are the typical thoughts that run through your mind when you love an addict. You can't understand why he continues on such a destructive path. Why does he make so many bad choices? Why does he cause so much pain to his family and loved ones?

It makes no sense that he continues to drink or take drugs even in the face of devastating consequences. He may know that you're going to leave him, that his children are hurting, that his job is on the line, that he is about to lose everything of value in his life, yet he can't seem to stop.

You get so angry because he obviously doesn't care. You blame him for being weak. But this isn't because he doesn't care and it's not because he's weak—he is sick with the disease of addiction. All of the blame, guilt, and arguing in the world won't change it. He needs help.

You expect him to ask for that help eventually. To seek it out once he hits "rock bottom". You believe that if you keep pointing out his mistakes, reminding him of his failures, and laying on the guilt, he will snap out of it and come to his senses. Unfortunately, for many addicts, it takes a tragic turn before they will reach out for help on their own.

You don't have the power to take addiction away from your loved one, but you do have the power to give him a good push toward help. You can get educated on addiction, talk to doctors, and find a good treatment program. Once you're ready, you can gather family and friends together and hold an intervention. You can give him an ultimatum.

An ultimatum—if you're serious and ready to follow through—may be all that it takes to convince him to accept help. If you decide to hold an intervention, however, you must be prepared. An intervention is not a confrontation, but if handled poorly it can turn into one. The smartest way to hold an intervention is with the help of a professional. Once you find a treatment program they can assist you with the process.

But before you are ready to do this, you may have to build your own mental and spiritual strength. That's what this book has been all about. You have to prepare yourself for the battle ahead. Addiction is cunning, strong, and fearless. You can't take on an opponent like that if you're lacking strength. If you do, it will find your weaknesses and use them against you.

My mental and spiritual strength was never tested so much as when I gave my husband an ultimatum. I told him that if he didn't go into treatment I was leaving him. When he refused to go, I had to gather all of my courage and move out. The weeks that followed were by far the toughest I had ever been through.

After sixteen years of marriage, he knew my insecurities. He was determined to scare me back home. He said things that in the past would have caused me to buckle. He threatened and harassed, believing that I would eventually give in. He broke and sold things of sentimental value—nothing was safe or sacred. But he underestimated my new strength. It was only after he realized that he couldn't break through my armor that he surrendered.

Had I not been working on my own inner strength, the

outcome would have been very different. I know that I would have given in because that's what I had done in the past. This wasn't the first time that I had given my husband an ultimatum, but it was the first time that I was prepared to follow through.

It's called tough love. It's making a stand against addiction and finally saying no to all of its madness. But there's a reason why it's called "tough," and it's just as hard on the family as it is on the addict. When you start to take on this new approach, you can become overwhelmed with guilt. It feels wrong, mean, and unloving.

I can remember him calling me and crying because he felt scared and alone. He would beg for me to come over just to hold him or keep him company. Saying no to him broke my heart. *"What kind of wife does that?"* I would ask myself. *"How can I say I love him but refuse to be there for him during his darkest hour?"*

Helping a loved one with addiction is very different from helping a loved one with any other illness. Anything that you do in order to ease his pain will only extend the disease, making it stronger. As long as you are going to be there to hold his hand, bail him out, fix his mistakes, and make life easier, he will never see the need to fight his disease.

That's why it's so important for families to understand addiction. The first step to helping your loved one is gaining knowledge. It's difficult to help another person if you don't understand the problem. That includes understanding what your role has been in enabling him.

If you were told that your child had diabetes you would learn everything you could about the disease. You would arm yourself with knowledge. You would stop buying sugary snacks, and you would probably make a lot of changes as a family in order to help your child with his or her battle. Like diabetes, addiction is a disease. By learning as much about addiction as possible, families can help their loved ones to recovery.

One of the best sources that I've found to help gain that knowledge is the book *Addiction. Why Can't They Just Stop?* It's based on an HBO documentary series. It combines over two years of research and reporting into a guide that covers the most up-to-date facts about addiction, new treatments, and hope. There are also endless resources at bookstores, libraries, and online.

In the process of learning about your loved one's addiction, don't lose sight of your own recovery and growth. By attending Al-Anon meetings, you can learn to make healthy changes in your family dynamic. You can gain strength and knowledge, not to mention the extra support of your group to help you through the rough times.

Even if you're not ready to face your loved one with an ultimatum yet, now is the time to find a good treatment program. This can be a daunting task. If you wait for the addict to say he's ready, in the time that it will take to finalize plans, he will likely change his mind. You'll want to have everything prepared so that when the time comes there are no delays.

Be forewarned—because of the privacy laws, it can be a struggle to get insurance companies and treatment programs to talk to you regarding your loved one's options. Many will respond by telling you that the addict needs to make this phone call himself. Don't be surprised if you hear the comment, "When he's ready to get help he'll seek it out on his own." It can be frustrating, but don't give up. Eventually you'll reach the right person—someone who understands the family's challenges and wants to help.

I can remember calling a treatment center and explaining my situation. I told the woman on the other line that I was looking for a program that my husband and I could afford and one that focuses on recovery for the entire family. She asked me why my husband wasn't making this phone call himself. I told her that he was too sick so I was taking matters into my own hands. I'll never forget her response. In a sarcastic tone, she told me, "Well, it sounds like you've got some real codependency issues. When he's ready to make this phone call himself you can give him the number. In the meantime why don't you get yourself some counseling?" I was speechless. Here I was attempting to find help for my husband, but I was left feeling ashamed and embarrassed. *Who are these people?* I thought. *And if they're working for a treatment center, why don't they understand?*

Fortunately, not everyone I spoke to was this insensitive. But as you make these phone calls yourself, be prepared for comments like these. It really goes to show how much ignorance there still is regarding addiction, even by so-called "experts in the field." Imagine a doctor telling you that when your diabetic child gets tired of being sick, she'll stop eating sugar.

Dealing with insurance companies and wading through all of the options can be complex and confusing. The addict is usually far too caught up in his addiction to face the phone calls and work involved in getting treatment arranged. For many addicts, just getting out of bed becomes overwhelming. If they are left to face the challenges of finding treatment, they may never get help.

A good place for the family to start their search is *The Substance Abuse Treatment Facility Locator* at www.findtreatment.samhsa.gov. This federal agency provides an online resource for locating drug and alcohol abuse treatment programs.

If you have insurance, of course you want to start there, but unfortunately, the majority of insurance companies fail to cover adequate treatment for addiction. Most cover medical detox, but there is usually a limit on how long (typically twenty-four to seventy-two hours). After that, the patient is released and expected to make it on willpower alone. The problem is that medical detox is only the beginning of treatment. It allows patients to get clean under medical supervision, but just because the drugs are no longer in their system doesn't mean that they're ready to face life drug-free. Without some type of rehabilitation they will likely relapse in a short time.

Some insurance companies will cover inpatient or outpatient programs, but it often depends on whether or not they find the treatment medically necessary. Be aggressive and persistent. Your insurance company may initially say no, but change their decision if you appeal.

An in-patient program typically lasts between twenty-one and ninety days. These programs are not cheap. The average cost is between $10,000 and $25,000 per month. Many experts recommend at least three months of in-patient care, so you can see how high the price tag can get, with no guarantee of success.

Out-patient programs cost significantly less and are more likely to be covered by insurance. Another benefit is that the patient can continue working, which for many households is a necessity. In these programs, the patient typically spends between two to eight hours a day in a group setting. The costs vary and many of these programs have financial assistance depending on the household's annual income.

Another option is seeing a physician, psychiatrist, psychologist, or counselor in a private setting. If this route is taken, it's important to find a person who is trained and has experience in substance abuse treatment. If the addiction involves opiates (Heroin, Methadone, Oxycodone, or Hydrocodone) a specialty physician can prescribe medication for treating opiate dependence.

Finances will most likely be a big factor in making a decision. According to the Substance Abuse and Mental Health Services Administration, 22.2 million Americans are addicted to drugs or alcohol, but ninety percent fail to get treatment. Studies show that the number one obstacle is cost. It's a sad fact that many families spend every bit of savings they have, including mortgaging their homes or draining retirement and college funds, in an attempt to save their loved one.

This is what leads many people to Alcoholics Anonymous and other twelve-step programs. They are free. They have meetings at many locations and at various times of the day. Thousands of people have used these programs to get clean and sober. For those who have completed a recovery program, AA can also be a good form of continuing care.

Keep in mind that every individual is different, and what

works for one person does not necessarily work for all. If your loved one tries this route and fails, it does not mean that the desire to quit isn't there.

For the family it's especially frustrating, because you want a program like AA to work. You don't want to clean out your bank account to pay for a treatment center. Life would be so much easier if your loved one could just work the twelve steps and get clean.

Then there is another issue for families to contend with—even if they come up with the funds needed to cover rehabilitation—seventy percent of patients relapse after their first time in treatment. It's not an easy fix. Recovery is a process that may include many relapses. This is a hard reality to face.

Once we convince the addict to go into treatment, we may feel a wave of relief. We think that finally the nightmare is over and now life can go back to normal. But we must be careful not to hold unrealistic expectations from treatment. There is no cure for addiction. For the addict, and for those who love the addict and choose to stand by him, recovery can be a lifelong battle.

Just recently I was forced to face this reality. After years of sobriety, my husband relapsed. He suffered a back injury and was prescribed pain medication. We both knew the risks, but he was in crippling pain, so I turned a blind eye and held out hope that he would be okay.

In a short time his prescription was increased and eventually changed to Oxycontin (a powerful pain killer that produces effects similar to heroin). Within a few weeks, he was completely hooked. He started taking higher doses than prescribed, which caused him to continually run out of medication. Desperate to stay high, he returned to drinking and smoking crack.

It was difficult to accept that after all the years of Dean's sobriety; his addiction was back as fiercely as ever. I really believed that this chapter of our lives was over, but here he was facing the same demon that he had seemingly overcome long ago. I now realize that it was never gone—just hiding out, waiting for the right opportunity to present itself.

With the help of our treatment center and family, we held an intervention. Dean went back through a recovery program and once again is feeling strong. I don't look at his relapse as a failure; instead I know that Dean has learned more about himself and his illness, and is another step closer to a life of sobriety. I pray that this was the last time he will need treatment, but I also know that recovery really is one day at a time.

I love the man who has returned to me clean and sober. The years before his relapse were truly wonderful, and I know that the years to come will be a beautiful gift as well. But I also realize that life is filled with ups and downs.

Addicts seem to get the concept of "one day at a time," but families tend to struggle with this. We want a contract, a promise, or a guarantee of a perfect future. We want the Norman Rockwell painting, but that is a lot of unfair pressure to put on our loved ones. To expect their sobriety to solve all of our problems and make the entire family whole is a tall order.

We must not forget that the addicts have a lot of work ahead of them. In most cases, the drugs and alcohol have been used to mask deeper issues that they will now need to face without the numbing effects of drugs. On top of that they will still have their cravings to deal with. Rehabilitation teaches addicts how to manage their addiction, but it cannot eliminate the desire.

Although recovery can be a rough road, it does not mean that relapse is inevitable. In fact, a promising statistic is that over half of the people who get treatment eventually reach a state of sustained recovery. But it is important to understand just how vulnerable the recovering addict can be even after years of sobriety. The real danger can come when the person believes that he's licked his addiction.

A good treatment program teaches the recovering addict how to stay away from situations that can lead to cravings, how to handle a bad day without turning to drugs or alcohol, and how to change his thinking when it's going in the wrong direction.

So what can the family do to improve the odds of their loved one's recovery? Education is the most important key. The family must understand the recovery process and the challenges that the addict will face.

It is vital that the home is a sober environment. If alcohol, prescription drugs, or illegal drugs are available in the home, then the odds of staying clean are slim to none. The entire household must be abstinent.

Family members should work on their own physical and emotional health. Each person must put their primary focus on themselves. It can be just as easy to get obsessed with the recovering addict as it was when he was using. Constantly looking for clues of relapse and waiting for him to mess up again will only harm his recovery. While it's true that trust is earned, we can easily push the addict back into old patterns if we're still holding onto resentment and punishing him for past mistakes.

This is why it's so important for family members to continue with their own recovery program. Support groups like Al-Anon are just as important once the addict goes into treatment. Sobriety can cause new strains on family relationships and this can be a challenging time for everyone. The healthiest way to handle these changes is for each person to stay focused on his or her own path.

I thank God that I was in the process of writing this book when Dean relapsed. My writing kept me focused and deterred me from the pitfalls of co-addiction. I'm so proud of myself for finding a way to nurture and protect my own desires, goals, and mental health in the face of my husband's addiction. This time I managed to avoid the obsession and self-pity that consumed me years before.

I had my dreams clear in my mind and I was moving toward them with or without him. That may sound selfish, but it was empowering. We each have choices to make. This was a crossroads for me. I could enter back into his world of addiction or I could move forward. He could come with me if he chose, but going back was no longer an option for me—I had come too far. I'm thankful that he chose to get more help and join me on the road to a healthy future.

While none of us chose this path consciously, a deeper love exists for the families that make it to the other side. In many ways we are lucky, because our eyes get opened to the simple joys in life that others may take for granted. The sound of laughter in our household becomes music. A Sunday afternoon together doing absolutely nothing is bliss. There is a bond that can only come from surviving a battle together. It is stronger and more profound than can ever be imagined. There is hope for our families. There is life after addiction.

Journaling Suggestion:

Take some time to go back and read through your journal. Have you already made some positive changes since starting this process? Do you feel stronger? Has your outlook improved? Are you having more fun? Write about your accomplishments. Every step toward health and happiness is worth celebrating. Along your new path you may feel some discomfort. Your stomach may flip-flop a bit as you try a new approach. The sensation of fear might spread throughout your body whenever you put yourself into an unfamiliar situation. It's important to stay in tune with your body's reactions, but sometimes it's hard to tell the difference between your instincts giving you a warning and the simple response to change. A natural reaction to change is fear, but many times this is a false warning. My sister has a name for these reactions—Growth Alerts. The next time you're feeling uneasy, ask yourself if there is a reason to be wary, or is it a signal that you are about to do some growing? Sometimes you have to push your way past the crowd of fear in order to reach the front row seats of joy.

It isn't for the moment you are stuck that
you need courage, but for the long uphill climb
back to sanity and faith and security.
-Henri Frederic Amiel

Just Say Yes

I believe that certain people come into your life right when you need them the most. They're like a special gift sent to teach you an important life lesson or help you to grow. Sandy was one of these people for me.

After staying home for eight years to be a full-time mom, I received a job offer that was hard to pass up. Sandy was a close friend of my mother-in-law's. She was working as a pharmacist at a local clinic and needed a pharmacy technician. Although I had no experience, and hadn't even applied or interviewed for the position, she was willing to hire me based on my mother-in-law's good word.

At first I wanted to turn the job down. I had been away from the outside world for so long that the thought of getting out there scared me. What if I didn't like it? What if I failed? Could I still be a good mom if I wasn't home all of the time? After much contemplation I chose to accept the position. I wasn't going to have any more children, and Jesse was eight years old. I knew that I couldn't hide out forever.

As soon as I started working, my fears were immediately dissolved. I learned quickly and became efficient. Sandy kept telling me how well I was doing and I thrived on the attention.

Being a full-time mom is a thankless position—you don't get paid, you never get promoted, and you rarely ever hear "thank you." I was finally getting some much needed recognition.

What I didn't expect was how much fun work could be. Although the days were long and often hectic, they were also filled with laughter and great times. There were just three of us working in the pharmacy—Sandy, Tammy (who also worked as a pharmacy technician), and me. Together we grew close and shared the most intimate details of our lives with each other. I had long ago lost touch with my former friends, so gaining these new friendships was an unexpected bonus that came with the job.

I grew especially close to Sandy. She was about fifteen years older than I, but had the kind of spirit and energy that made me feel like the older one. Sandy was like no one else I had ever met. Not only was she warm and giving (which was probably why she had an amazing number of friends), but she also had a sense of adventure that filled her days with everything from rock climbing to skydiving.

Sandy was married but did not have any children. While she understood the demands that motherhood brought, she did not sympathize with the demands I felt from my husband. When I turned down invitations to do things after work or on the weekends, she would frown on the fact that I had no extracurricular activities. Going to work was really the only thing I did away from my family.

One Friday, as the work day was coming to an end, Sandy asked me what my plans were for the weekend. I told her that I had nothing special going on. "Well, tomorrow morning I want you to come with me." She said. "I'm helping some friends set up their hot air balloons and since you have no plans you can join us."

I felt trapped. "No, I can't." I insisted. "Dean has plans in the morning so I have to take care of my son." That was a lie—Dean had no plans that I knew of—but it seemed like a good excuse.

"Bring your son with you." Sandy responded. "He'll have fun. I'm not taking no for an answer. There's absolutely no reason for you not to go." She then proceeded to give me directions to the site where they would be meeting.

On my drive home that night, I was anxious. I knew that Sandy was right, but she was pushing me to do something I wasn't comfortable with. My weekends were always for my family. This would be the first time that I had made plans without discussing them first with Dean. I didn't want him to use this as an excuse to start an argument or go out and get high.

As I thought more about it, though, I got angry. Dean obviously had no problem making plans without me. He didn't consider my feelings every time he disappeared for the night leaving me to worry. I deserved to have some fun. By the time I got home, I was ready to stand up to Dean and tell him how it was. But, to my surprise, when I told Dean my plans his reaction was very different from what I had expected.

"That's fine," he said "because I have to work in the morning." That was it. No big tantrum. No guilt trip. It was then I realized that Dean had never held me back; that was something that I did to myself.

Jesse and I had an early start the next day. We had to be there at six in the morning and the location was an hour away from our home. As we hit the road, my eyes burned and I wished I was back in my warm bed. Jesse slept in the passenger seat next to me as I fueled up with a cup of coffee.

The sun was just coming up as we pulled into the large clearing of land where the group was gathering. We found Sandy and she put us right to work. There was a lot of preparation involved in getting the balloons ready for flight. As they started to fill with air and come alive, the scene was magical. There were about ten balloons, and they were each magnificent as they slowly grew in size and towered above us. I watched Jesse looking at them with total amazement, and immediately felt grateful that I was able to share this moment with him.

As they began to take off, one of Sandy's friends called for me to join her in her balloon. "I can't," I said. "I have my son here."

"Don't be silly," Sandy said. "Jesse will be fine with me. How often do you get a chance to take a ride in a hot air balloon?"

"Go, mom," Jesse insisted, pushing me towards the balloon. He was so excited that you'd think he was the one being invited for a ride.

"Well, alright, why not," I said as a couple of people helped me into the basket. As we began to lift off the ground, adrenaline was surging through my body. Standing close to Sandy, Jesse waved to me with a giant smile on his face. "Goodbye Toto, goodbye Scarecrow," I jokingly called to them as I waved back.

It was an exhilarating feeling as we lifted higher and higher into the sky. Each of the balloons kept a safe distance from the others as we drifted slowly along. I always thought that a hot air balloon ride would be scary. It turned out to be more peaceful than I had expected. We didn't talk much while we were up there. Instead we quietly took in the views, and for some reason that I don't really understand myself, I grew emotional.

I thought about what an unexpected surprise this was. Little did I know when I woke up that morning that I would be taking a ride in a hot air balloon. Had Sandy not pushed me past my comfort zone, I would have said no and missed out on this opportunity. Up in that balloon I gained a new perspective. I felt so alive and free. I couldn't help but wonder how many times saying "no" had kept me from enjoying life's adventures.

After drifting for a few miles, we started to descend. I could see Jesse and Sandy below, along with the rest of the crowd. They had traveled to a second clearing where all the balloons would be landing.

Once we were back on the ground, everyone worked on getting the balloons and equipment packed up. Afterwards, we enjoyed hot dogs and an assortment of potluck dishes while music blasted from a car stereo. People were dancing and laughing, and I remember thinking that this was one of the fullest days that I had ever experienced—and it was only ten in the morning!

The day before I had been fearful of accepting Sandy's invitation—but why? Why did I feel this need to avoid new situations? Why did I walk around on eggshells so much of the time? My fears had turned out to be false. It was time to stop saying "no."

We're told that we need to learn to say "no" more often. Take a look at the bookstore shelves in the self-help section and you'll find an array of titles such as, *How to Say No, The Power of a Positive No, 250 Ways to Say No,* and many more, all with the goal of teaching us how to say no. And while it's true that we need to set healthy boundaries in our lives, we also need to learn to say "yes" to those opportunities that come along and offer us the chance to live more fully.

For those of us living with an addict, we tend to say no too often out of fear. If the day is going well, we become afraid of upsetting some delicate balance. We don't want to do anything that might rock the boat. If we just don't move, don't talk, don't breathe, then everything might be okay.

We need to let go of our attempts at controlling the decisions and actions of others. As we learn to live our own lives and follow our own paths, we lead the way for our loved ones. It is up to them whether or not they join us.

So what if your loved one doesn't choose to join you? It's likely that your main objective has been finding a way to save the addict in your life. Focusing on your own needs has not been the priority. But it is by focusing on yourself that you create the healthiest possible environment for your loved one to choose sobriety. Regardless of what you do, though, his decision about how to live his life is ultimately up to him.

Your happiness is not dependent on your loved one's recovery. As you start to say yes to new opportunities, as you take steps toward health, as you learn to detach from the problems of addiction, you will change. Your dreams of the future may evolve as well. You may discover that your desire to save your relationship with the addict has weakened. People change and grow apart. More than anything, you may feel the need to move on. These feelings can cause a lot of confusion and guilt.

You might try to ignore these changes happening inside of you. So much time, love, and effort have been poured into your relationship that you can't fathom letting it go. You may choose to stay your course and battle for the dreams that you've worked so hard for.

But sometimes all the planning, praying, and determination in the world can't get you to the place you want to go. The current you're swimming against is just too strong and is pulling you in the opposite direction. You may have to stop fighting against it and let go.

Letting go does not mean that you're giving up. It's more of a surrendering process. Sometimes you grow too attached to a dream or an idea. You end up limiting yourself because you won't open your mind to another way. Letting go may require some time for grieving. But as the pain subsides, you will create space for something new to enter your life. Possibly the very thing you dreamed of having in the first place.

This is what happened for me when I left my husband. As much as I yearned for my marriage to work, I finally surrendered to the fact that he was not ready to accept help. I did what I had to do to save myself and walked away. It was only after I gained the courage to take those steps that my husband accepted recovery.

That's not to say that the addict in your life will do the same. We are each living with our own unique circumstances. You could find that even if sobriety is achieved, the wounds are too deep to heal properly. The scars left behind might be too ugly to ignore. When a marriage or relationship ends we tend to see it as a failure—but there is no such thing as a failed relationship.

Every relationship in your life, and every situation has helped to mold you into the person you are today. You are an ever-evolving, learning, growing, changing creation. I've heard it said that your soulmate is the person who pushes you the hardest to learn and grow. Your soulmate could possibly be the one who has hurt you the most. Through that pain, you may have learned your greatest lessons.

Relationships evolve. Sometimes you hold on to a vision of what your love was like in the beginning. In reality, you are both different people now. It can never be exactly as it was. I know from my own experience that love can heal and grow deeper. But just as love can heal, it can also fade away. Over time everything changes. Whether your love strengthens or weakens, it will never stay the same.

Only you can make the decision as to whether or not to end your relationship with the addict. Not your family, your friends, a book, or a counselor. You must follow your own heart and your own instincts. Leaving can be the most difficult decision you make in your life, but it may be the only way that you can find your own peace and happiness.

It is heartbreaking to walk away. I know, because I did it once. Regardless of how much pain the addict may have caused you over the years, you want to protect him from feeling that same hurt. But sometimes, it is only through a great deal of pain that healing can occur.

Sadly, you may be the only one who eventually heals. You could lose your loved one to his disease. By taking your own steps away from the nightmare of addiction, you open a doorway for the addict. You give him the opportunity to see the light shining through. You can encourage him, you can offer hope and help, you can lead by example, but you can not take his steps for him.

I feel fortunate that Dean has accepted help. Today he is clean. But tomorrow, next week, or next year, he may be struggling again. Just as Dean must work to stay clean every day, I must work on my own recovery from co-addiction.

I've discovered that when you take the focus off the addict and put it back onto yourself, you no longer have so much fear. You come to realize that you are in control of your own destiny. You can build new relationships, discover new hobbies, find time to play, and set goals for yourself outside of your relationship with the addict.

There is no other person in this world who can make you happy. Only you can do that for yourself. You are in a relationship with an addict, but it is only one of many relationships in your life. Accept the personal gifts that each person has to offer, give back to them your special gifts, and accept that we are each imperfect human beings trying to make our way.

You have within you the power to create the life of your dreams. By detaching from the problems of addiction and taking control of your own life; by making your mental and physical health a top priority; by getting in touch with your spirituality; by setting your own goals and clearly envisioning your bright future; by learning as much as you can about addiction and the role that you've been playing; and by reaching out for help and guidance, you become the architect of your life. And in the process, you will be helping to create the best possible environment for your loved one to accept help.

Life is a journey full of surprises, beautiful scenery, great loves, and wonderful treasures. It is also filled with battles, uphill climbs, and many detours—these are all a part of the journey.

It's time to let go of false fears and say "yes." No matter what happens—when you can find peace within yourself—you will be okay. Learn to say yes to fun, adventure, new friendships, and taking risks. There are no perfect answers, perfect relationships, or perfect lives. We are meant to make mistakes, take wrong turns, and make bad decisions. They are all a part of life. Just say yes—yes to love, yes to learning, yes to growing, yes to life.

My wish for you: all of the happiness in the world—you deserve it!

Happiness is not in our circumstances,
but in ourselves. It is not something we see,
like a rainbow, or feel, like the heat of a fire.
Happiness is something we are.
                    -John B Sheerin

Resources

Al-Anon/Alateen:
888-4AL-ANON / 757-563-1600
www.al-anon.alateen.org

Alcoholics Anonymous (AA):
Check your phone book for local listings.
www.alcoholics-anonymous.org

Narcotics Anonymous (NA):
818-997-3822
www.na.org

Nar-Anon:
www.alcoholism.about.com/od/naranon

National Domestic Violence/Abuse Hotline:
1-800-799-SAFE (7233) or 1-800-787-3224
www.ndvh.org

The Substance Abuse Treatment Facility Locator:
www.findtreatment.samhsa.gov

Center for Substance Abuse Treatment (CSAT):
240-276-2750
www.csat.samhsa.gov

**National Institute on Alcohol Abuse
and Alcoholism (NIAAA):**
301-443-3860
www.niaaa.nih.gov

Soaring Above Co-Addiction Website:
www.soaringabovecoaddiction.com

Suggested Reading

Why Don't They Just Quit?, Joe Herzanek

The Language of Letting Go, Melody Beattie

Journey to the Heart, Melody Beattie

Addiction, Why Can't They Just Stop, Hoffman & Froemke

Getting Them Sober, Toby Rice Drews

Addict in the Family, Beverly Conyers

Manifest Your Destiny, Wayne Dyer

The Seven Spiritual Laws of Success, Depok Chopra

The Courage to be Rich, Susie Orman

Do What You Love, the Money Will Follow, Marsha Sinetar

The Automatic Millionaire, David Bach

Meditations, Shakti Gawain

Creative Visualization, Shakti Gawain

Simple Abundance, Sarah Ban Breathnach

Feel the Fear and Do It Anyway, Susan Jeffers, Ph.D.

**Be sure to visit *www.soaringabovecoaddiction.com*
for continued inspiration and support.**

About the Author

Lisa Espich lives in Tucson, Arizona, with her husband, Dean. They are surrounded by a supportive and loving family, which includes their son, Jesse. Lisa is a successful manager and coach for a Fortune 500 company. *Soaring Above Co-Addiction* is her debut book. After creating her own personal program for recovery from co-addiction, and witnessing the remarkable transformation by her husband, she is now passionate about helping other families to heal from the devastating effects of addiction. Lisa has designed a workshop based on the principles shared in her book. If you would like to find out more about her workshops please go to www.soaringabovecoaddiction.com.

Give the Gift of Hope and Inspiration to Your Loved Ones and Friends

❑ YES, I would like _____ copies of Soaring Above Co-Addiction at $14.95 each, plus $5 shipping per book. Please allow up to 14 days for delivery.

❑ YES, I would like each copy autographed by the author at no additional charge to the following name(s):

_____

_____

My check or money order for $ _____ is enclosed.

Please charge my:

❑ Visa # _____

❑ MasterCard # _____

❑ American Express # _____

Exp Date _____ Signature _____

Name _____

Address _____

City/State/Zip _____

Phone _____ Email_____

Please make your check payable and mail to:
Twin Feather Publishing
P.O. Box 18910
Tucson, Az 85731
ot fax to: 520-721-6782